THE ADVENTURES OF JACOB & LISA

DISCOVERY

JAY VERNON

Illustrated by
COURTNEY DILWORTH

HANGAR 1 PUBLISHING

THE ADVENTURES OF JACOB & LISA

This is a fantastical tale of discovery by two eleven-year-old friends in the woods of Jacob's farm in central Wisconsin. Through tragedy and their curiosity of nature, they find that their world is full of mystery and folklore that leaves them with more questions than answers. Tag along with Jacob, Lisa, and their friends as their knowledge of their world and what is true is tested at every turn.

INTRODUCTION
SUMMER BEGINS

Today was extremely exciting for Jacob because it was the first day off school and summer finally began. Jacob liked school but his favorite thing to do is be outside on their farm with the animals and nature. On the farm were cows, chickens and two horses. Jacob's chores every morning and night is to feed and water all the animals. Cleaning out their pens and brushing the horses are also his responsibility. Living on the farm is demanding work but Jacob loved the open spaces and investigating all the wild animals that also called the one hundred seventy-five-acre farm their home. Besides the domesticated farm animals, there are squirrels, chipmunks, rabbits, deer, raccoons, several types of birds and even a family of red foxes that have dug out a den and live on the hillside above the apple orchard. Jacob even named many of these animals and would also have conversations with them, anytime he encountered them. This was most likely attributed to the fact that Jacob was an only child and spent much of his time by himself. So, all the creatures Jacob encountered were part of his family and also considered them to be his friends.

To help support the family, Jacob's father worked in the nearby town as a farm equipment repairperson. With so many farms nearby there was lots of work for his father, therefore his father spent most days away from the farm. Even Jacob had to work on the weekend. The farm animals needed food and water seven days a week. That is the life of a family on any type of farm.

Jacob's mother had a part time job in town working a few hours a day at a dress shop sewing and selling dresses. The dress shop was where the ladies around town would meet to chitchat about the latest gossip. Jacob's mother would then repeat all the stories to Jacob's father at dinner and he would in turn tell her the stories that he had heard at the tractor shop. Sometimes the stories would match but not very often. Jacob usually didn't pay much attention since most of their conversations were usually about the adults in town. Many nights Jacob would always hurry to eat his meal and then visit with the animals until bedtime. Even though he loved both his parents very much, Jacob preferred talking to the animals.

Making conversation with the horses is much more interesting than listening to his parents. Even if the animals didn't usually answer back. However, there were several occasions when Jacob could swear that the animals could understand him and were replying to his words.

1

WOLF

While Jacob was brushing the horses tonight, he saw something hairy flash by the side of the barn. It was dark, so Jacob quickly grabbed a flashlight they kept hanging by the barn doors for emergencies and started searching around the outside of the barn. Whatever had run by him was really fast. Jacob then heard a noise in the small apple grove behind the barn. It sounded like a twig snapping and an animal breathing heavily. Suddenly, something ran past his light and darted off deeper into the apple grove. He didn't know what this was but the first thing that came to his mind was maybe it was a wolf. Jacob's father had recently told a story at dinner that a neighboring farm had seen a wolf on his property. Fear then set into Jacob's mind as he retreated toward the house. Jacob ran into the house and yelled "I think there's a wolf out in the apple grove!"

Both Jacob's mother and father came running to see what all the commotion was about. Jacob, out of breath, repeated himself, "I think there's a wolf in the apple grove!"

Jacob's mother gasped while his father turned immediately and grabbed his shotgun from the gun cabinet. Jacob's father commanded, "You both stay in the house!" He then ran outside with the gun and flashlight to chase away the wolf. A wolf, that brazen, could hurt, or even kill their farm animals.

After a few minutes Jacob and his mother heard a knock at the front door. Jacob's mother opened the door slowly. Standing there was Lisa, one of Jacob's classmates who lived just down the road. Jacob's mother then told Lisa to quickly get inside.

Once inside Lisa asked, "What is going on?"

Jacob's mother said, "Jacob's father is outside hunting for a wolf in the apple grove."

Lisa replied, "A wolf?"

Wolf

Jacob stepped in and said, "Yes, I think I saw a wolf while I was with the horses in the barn."

Lisa screamed in panic "Noooo! That's my dog Rio!" She got out of our yard and ran this way!"

Jacob's mouth dropped open as he looked in shock at his mother. Jacob yelled "We have to let father know." Jacob and Lisa ran out the door toward the barn yelling to his father. "Don't shoot! It's Lisa's dog Rio!"

Jacob's father came out of the orchard and was relieved to find out it was a false alarm. Lisa had tears in her eyes, when out from the other side of the barn came running to her feet, her dog, Rio. Lisa hugged her dog and then hugged Jacob tightly in relief that Rio was ok.

Jacob and his father climbed into their truck and drove Lisa and Rio back to their house. Lisa's mom and dad were outside waiting for the two of them. After a short conversation between my father and her parents, Lisa surprised me by giving me another big hug before running into her house with Rio. Lisa's love for her dog reminded me of my love for our animals on the farm.

As we made our way back home, my father commented, "You had better get to bed because we have a lot of work to get done this weekend."

2

TRIMMING TREES

Today I woke up to my father's voice, "Jacob, time to get up. We've got lots of work to do." Usually, my mother was the one to wake me. My father wanted to get a good head start with all the work we have ahead of us today. As I walked out of my room my mother was putting my favorite breakfast of pancakes, bacon, scrambled eggs, and fresh biscuits on the table. As I wiped the sleep from my eyes my mother said, "Good morning, Jacob."

I replied excitedly, "Good morning! Breakfast smells great and I am starving!"

My father was already outside loading the trailer with the chainsaw, axes, bow saws, gas, and oil for the chainsaw. My mother was packing water and snacks for us since we were going to be up in the woods working most of the day.

I was so excited to work with my father all weekend! He was always teaching me about how to properly do things. He would say, "If you're going to do something, you might as well do it right the first time. Otherwise, you'll be doing it over again." It can be frustrating sometimes to learn the correct way of doing certain tasks, but it always was easier the more times I would try.

Pancakes, eggs and bacon

I quickly finished my breakfast and headed outside to meet with my father who was waiting for me. He started the truck and we drove up the trail that leads into our woods. My father followed the trail for about one mile. At the end was a turnabout. My father parked the truck and threw me a brand-new pair of work gloves and said, "You're going to need these!"

As a big smile grew on my face and I replied, "Thanks!"

My father and I grabbed all the equipment needed out of the truck and set up a little work area on the tailgate. My job was to drag away any branches that he cut off the trees and pile them up. There were several trees that were dead and had fallen. We cut those up first. Then my father wanted to extend the trail further into the woods, so he started cutting smaller live trees down to make room for us to drive through. Before we could do that, we needed to dig out the stumps. That is always the hardest and most time-consuming part of clearing a path.

I could hear my mother who was bringing up the tractor to help pull out the bigger tree stumps. As she drove around the corner, I could see to my surprise that Lisa was riding on the tractor as well. They were both smiling from ear to ear. It would be nice having someone my age around, plus we would be able to get more work done. My father had Lisa and I shovel the dirt from around the stumps and then my father would hook a big log chain around it and yank the stumps out. Then he would use the front bucket on the tractor to level out the ground for the trail. I was really enjoying myself as we worked as a family. Having Lisa helping us was a bonus, except when she would throw the dirt from her hole around the stump into the area where I was digging. She would act like it was accidental, but I knew she was being silly.

My mother then yelled to us from behind the truck where she had set up a folding table, "I have everyone's lunch ready!" We all dropped what we were doing, loaded up our plates, and sat on a fallen tree to eat. Working so hard really makes a person hungry. My parents talked and laughed about how much Lisa and I were so cute together. Lisa smiled and started to blush. I, on the other hand, wasn't amused by the conversation as it made me rather uncomfortable. I thought of Lisa as one of my friends, just like any other male friend of mine. I jumped up and decided it would be best if I just got back to work. My mother said, "Don't worry Lisa, he'll come around, some day." My parents laughed and Lisa's face turned red again. I chose to ignore her comment and continued working.

As my father was picking up a log he yelled out in pain. He had gotten a large splinter in his hand. My mother looked at it and decided she would need to get a pair of tweezers and a band aid. My father said to her, "I'll go back to the house with you. It'll be quicker." My father then told us, "Stay near the truck. If there is any sort of danger, you both need to get into the truck and lock the doors!" Lisa and I shook our heads in agreement. Neighbors have seen black bears and an occasional mountain lion in the area, but not very often. My father always kept his rifle in the truck for protection in case we ever ran into one.

Once they left, Lisa and I kept picking up branches and cleaning up the area. I grabbed the axe and started chopping down several of the very small trees that were in the way of the new path.

Lisa then said, "Stop, do you hear that?"

I said, "Hear what?"

She replied, "It sounds like someone is chopping wood further back into the woods!"

I listened for a minute and sure enough, there were three chops in a row. It sounded like it was coming from the very back of our woods.

Lisa said, "We should go check it out!"

I said "No, my father had told both of us to stay close to the truck!"

Lisa was persistent. She grabbed my hand tightly and pulled me toward where the chopping noises were coming from. She excitedly said, "Don't worry, we'll be back before your father returns."

I was reluctant but decided to follow her.

As we quickly walked, we heard the chopping noise again. I then quietly said to Lisa, "Slow down and walk quietly!"

We started to tip toe when we heard the chopping noise once again! It was remarkably close now. Lisa was now squeezing my hand very tightly. As we climbed to the top of a small hill and peered down into a ravine, we could see an exceptionally large dark figure behind a bunch of trees. We couldn't make out what it was.

Lisa, quietly said "We should move closer." As she started to get up, we heard three more loud chops. It was coming from the ravine. As we laid there wondering what to do next, we heard the truck horn from behind us. My father had made it back already.

We looked at each other and I said "Way to go Lisa! We are in trouble now! We better hurry and get back!"

Out of nowhere was this loud grunt from the ravine. We both looked and then out from behind the tree stepped a huge hairy beast walking on two feet. We froze for a second in shock! Then Lisa let out this blood curdling scream. The beast had seen us and out of its rage it broke a small tree in half and threw it in our direction. I then grabbed her hand and started running back toward the truck as fast as we could. I could hear what sounded like a freight train crashing through the trees behind us. I looked back to see if it was gaining on us. Suddenly, I tripped. As I fell, I hit my head pretty hard and was injured. Lisa stopped and was screaming for me to get up. That's when I passed out.

3

WHERE AM I?

The next time I remember anything was that my head was killing me. I must have hit my head very hard and now I am suffering from a concussion. I could tell that it was dark out and I was very cold. I could sense that there was someone bustling around me, but I couldn't see anything. I tried to speak but couldn't get any words out. I think I was just mumbling. At that time, I passed out again.

Sometime later I woke up again. My head was still badly hurting. There was a very pungent smell in the air that was making me very nauseous. As I opened my eyes, I could tell that it was now daylight, but everything was still very blurry. I could hear something grunting a short distance away. It sounded like an animal and not a person. Fear then started running through my body. What was it? A wolf? A bear? I tried to sit up, but it made my head hurt worse. I tried to move but I couldn't find the strength. I could hear heavy footsteps approaching me. I was in fear that this could be it for me. I opened my eyes even though I was afraid of what was coming my way. My eyes were so blurry that I could only make out a big dark mass that knelt down on the ground next to me. This must be my father. I was only able to get out one word, "Dad?"

The trail into the woods

There was no response. Then a big sigh and grunt. This was definitely not my father. Then suddenly I was being picked up off the ground. The smell was so bad I could barely keep it down.

I was able to get out a few words and I asked, "Who are you?"

Again, there was no response. I could barely see a face. It was very dark and hairy. Then I realized that I wasn't in a person's arms. I was almost sure that I was in the arms of what Lisa, and I had seen. I tried to get free, but this creature had me secured tightly in its arms. I could feel it's large, hairy arms and its breath was hot and smelled like a dead animal. For some reason I knew what the creature was thinking. It wasn't talking as far as I could tell. Yet, I had this feeling that it wasn't going to hurt me. Then suddenly it stopped dead in its tracks. The forest was now totally quiet. Then, in the distance, I could hear my father's voice, calling my name. The first thing I thought of was that he was walking into danger. What would happen if my father saw this creature? I just wanted to get to my father so I started to yell as loud as I could, "Help me!"

The creature gently set me down on the ground. I could tell it started thrashing a tree back and forth. Maybe it was trying to scare my father off? Then I could hear its heavy footsteps as it ran away quickly back deeper into the forest.

My father's voice grew louder. "Jacob! Where are you?"

I yelled, "Over, hear, over here!" It was all I could do to get those words out as loud as I could.

My father spotted me and ran to me. He knelt down beside me. He was really shaken up. His voice was trembling, "Jacob are you ok?"

I warned him that there was a big creature nearby.

He replied in frustration, "You kids need to stop with the scary creature story."

I said, "I'm not lying. Lisa saw it too! It chased us and I fell and hit my head." Then I asked, "Is Lisa, ok?"

He said, "Yes, she's ok. Lisa told us you were both being chased by a Bigfoot and that you fell, and she kept running. We looked all night in these woods for you."

I replied, "The creature took me to their camp, cared for me and set me here when it heard your voice."

My father in protest said, "I've heard enough about monsters! We need to get you to the hospital right away!"

My father picked me up and carried me to a path where he had his horse waiting. My father said as he picked me up, "Whew, you need a bath son!" I agreed! I did notice that my father struggled to carry me versus how easy it was for the creature to pick me up and carried me much further than my father had. My father was out of breath as well.

We met my mother at the house. She was hysterical with tears running down her face. My father threw me into the truck and raced off towards the hospital.

Once at the hospital the doctors checked me out and said that I was a lucky young man. The doctor then announced that I had a very bad concussion but that I was expected to make a full recovery. The doctor said that my blurry eyesight will slowly go back to normal, and my headache should also go away with fluids and a couple days of rest.

Just then I heard someone entering the room yelling my name. "Jacob! Jacob! You're alive!" It was Lisa with tears in her eyes. She leaned over the bed and hugged me so tightly that it hurt.

I let out a big "Aaahhhh!"

Lisa let go and then proceeded to yell at me, "Don't you ever scare me like that ever again!" Then she gave me a kiss on the cheek and whispered, "We can't tell anyone what we saw. They'll never believe us." I painfully nodded my head in agreement. Lisa then added as she stood up, "OMG Jacob! You need a bath! You really stink!"

Lisa's sign for Jacob

My mother came back into the room after talking to one of the doctors out in the hallway and said to me, "Since your concussion is bad Jacob, just to be safe, they are going to keep you overnight."

My father spoke, "I can stay here tonight with Jacob."

Unexpectedly, Lisa stood up and in a very authoritative voice, "This is all my fault. I'll stay with Jacob."

My parents looked at each other and my mom asked Lisa, "Let's check with your parents first." Lisa agreed. My mother called Lisa's mother and she said it would be ok for her to stay.

After everyone left and the doctors were all gone for the day, it was time for Lisa and me to discuss what happened.

The first thing that came out of her mouth was, "Oh my God Jacob, we saw a Bigfoot!"

I quickly replied, "At least you didn't have to camp overnight with them!"

Lisa responded with, "What? There was more than one?"

I said, "Yes, I couldn't see them due to my eyesight and it was dark, but I believe there were at least two. Maybe even three."

Lisa was in complete shock. Lisa asked, "A whole family of them?"

I said, "I think so. They took care of me and one of them put some sort of tree bark in my mouth and poured water from a big leaf a couple times."

Lisa replied, "So they were taking care of you? Kinda like the doctors have been doing here in the hospital?"

I replied, "I guess so."

Lisa stood up and said, "That's amazing!"

I then told her how one of them picked me up, carried me, and shook the tree so that my father could find me. Lisa was absolutely amazed and kept probing for more information about what had happened. She wanted to know more but I was starting to fall asleep from my medicines.

She said, "You get some rest, and we'll discuss this more once you get home."

4

BACK HOME

The next morning, I was released from the hospital and arrived home with my mother. To my surprise, sitting, waiting on the front steps, was Lisa.

My mother said with a giggle and a smile, "Looks like you have a girlfriend."

I replied in a dissatisfied demeanor, "Hardly mother!"

My mother just kept smiling and said, "I'm going to fix you all some breakfast. Make sure you invite her to stay." Before I could get out a word my mother nodded her head and said, "Yes! You must!" It was like she could read my mind.

As I got out of the car, Lisa yelled out, "Welcome home Jacob!" She even had a sign that said, "Glad you're alive!" I guess I kinda sneered and started to walk by her. I was a little grumpy and really wasn't in the mood for visitors today.

Then my mother spoke up and asked, "Lisa, Jacob was hoping you would stay for breakfast."

Lisa excitedly replied, "I would love to! Thank you!"

As my mother was cooking breakfast, Lisa and I sat in the front room. Lisa was instantly asking questions left and right. I couldn't keep up with her. She wanted to go into the woods as soon as we were done eating breakfast.

I said, "No way! I'm not going up there ever again!"

Lisa jumped up from the couch and asked, "Are you scared? The creature took care of you! It even brought you back to your father! Let's go see if it's still around!" Lisa stopped long enough, and I was finally able to say something.

"I'm quite sure there was more than one. Maybe even a family of three. A mom, dad, and child. I couldn't really tell since my eyesight was too blurry to see anything other than silhouettes."

Lisa couldn't believe it! "A whole family of creatures in your woods?" She asked.

"All I know is that these creatures are considered folklore. No one has ever proven one hundred percent that they exist. Yet, here, we both saw it and I was taken care of by them at their campsite. No one is going to believe us. Unless we could get proof, Lisa!" We could hear my mother calling us for breakfast.

My mother had quite a sense of humor. She made pancakes that looked like big feet with all the toes even. I almost didn't want to eat them. I mean, who really wants to eat something that looks like a foot.

Lisa had a chuckle as did my mother. Lisa asked with a giggle, "What? Too soon, Jacob?"

My mother asked as she served us some bacon and eggs, "What are you two up to today?"

Lisa quickly replied, "I'm going to make sure Jacob gets plenty of rest."

My mother responded with, "Awe! That's so sweet of you, Lisa. I must run to town and get some supplies. If you two need anything, just give me a call."

Lisa smiled and nodded. As soon as my mother started the car, Lisa grabbed my hand and said, "Let's go find your friends!"

I annoyingly asked, "You want to go back into the woods?"

Lisa excitedly replied, "Yes! Let's take my smartphone and try to get a picture of them! We would be famous!"

I told her, "I really don't want to be famous. Especially for a subject like Bigfoot. We would be ridiculed and never be a part of the cool kids!"

Lisa grabbed my arm and pulled me out the door and down the front steps. As we headed up the hill toward the woods, I started to get somewhat scared. I know deep down that I didn't want to necessarily run into this creature again. Even though I feel it had cared for me that night, I wasn't sure it wanted us to be bothering them. Maybe next time we did, that it might not end well.

Lisa kept pulling me toward the woods. She wasn't being very quiet.

I said to her, "Hey, you need to be very quiet if we're going to have any luck finding them."

Lisa looked at me and nodded her head in agreement. We quietly proceeded toward the area where my father found me. As we started to get close, we could smell something very rancid. Lisa and I made a stinky face toward each other. We reached a ledge that overlooked a ravine with a small creek that runs through the middle of it. I signaled to Lisa to stay low because I heard a noise across from us on the other side of the ravine. Lisa then pointed across the ravine at a group of small pines. All I could see was some of the branches moving. There was no wind. So, it couldn't be that. Then a dark figure could be seen through some of the branches. I still couldn't make out what it is. Lisa then signaled with her hand for us to move to a better vantage point higher on the ridge. I put my finger on my lips to signal to her to be very quiet. Lisa nodded once again in agreement.

As we made our way I stepped on a branch, and it made a loud snap. We both froze. Suddenly there was a grunt and rustling from behind the pines that we had seen moving. Lisa and I looked at each other in fear that we had been seen. We ducked down and laid still as possible. Our hearts were beating out of our chests. At that point I felt we needed to get out of there. I then motioned to Lisa that we should get back to the farm. She nodded head once again in agreement. As we started to sneak away, Lisa caught her shirt on a branch and broke it. It made a loud snap that could be heard from far away. Then we heard a loud roar from the valley. We looked at each other in fear. You could hear whatever was crashing through the trees toward us.

I yelled, "Run!"

We both ran as fast as we could. My head started to really hurt, and I had to stop.

Lisa in a panicked voice yells at me, "What are you doing? We have to get out of here!" I tried to get back up to my feet but just couldn't. Lisa grabbed my hand and tried to help me up. We could hear heavy footsteps approaching us. Lisa yelled, "We have to go!" Then suddenly Lisa went limp and passed out.

I yelled, "Lisa! Lisa! Are you ok?" I could hear something breathing heavily behind me. I slowly turned my head and couldn't believe my eyes. It was the creature standing only ten feet away staring down at us! It must have had to be eight to nine feet tall! I tried shaking Lisa to wake her, but she was limp. The creature grunted a couple times and started to walk away. I tried to lift Lisa up but couldn't. My head was pounding. I didn't know how we were going to get out of here. I then heard footsteps walking up behind me once again.

As I turned, I could see it was the creature. I panicked and yelled at the creature, "Leave us alone! Go away!"

The creature just looked at me and came closer.

I yelled again, "Leave us alone!" I got between Lisa and the creature.

The creature reached around me and started to pick Lisa up off the ground.

I didn't want the creature to touch her, so I yelled. "Don't touch her!" I grabbed its long hairy arm and tried to pull it away from Lisa with literally no effect.

The creature was too strong. I could hear in my head, "I won't hurt her." I again, did not hear any words being spoken out loud. As the creature picked Lisa up, I heard it once again. "I will not hurt her."

The creature carrying Lisa

The creature held Lisa on its chest like a parent would hold a sleeping child. The creature then reached down, grabbed me by the arm and pulled me up into its other arm. The creature then looked me in the eyes and snorted. I then remembered how it had cared for me before.

I then pointed toward the farm and said, "Home."

The creature hesitated and then let out a loud, "Whoop!" that rang in my ears! Then from the woods I heard another whoop. The creature whooped again and started walking in the direction of the farm. I wasn't sure if it was taking us home or not.

I started to feel at ease when I could hear in my head, "You are safe. I will take you both to your home." I almost felt as though I was going crazy. How can I be hearing something without any words being said?

As we reached the edge of the woods and our corn field, the creature stopped and looked around. I think the creature was weary of being out in the open. There was a row of hickory trees along the edge of the apple orchard that I pointed at that led to the back of the barn. The creature seemed to understand and started heading toward the row of trees. As we approached the back of the barn, the creature put us gently down.

Lisa was starting to slowly wake. She opened her eyes and started to scream.

I quickly covered her mouth with my hand. I could hear my mother pulling into the driveway. I looked at the creature and said, "Thank you!"

The creature snorted and quickly made his way back to the woods. I could swear that I heard the creature say, "You're welcome." I then peaked around the corner of the garage checking for my mother. She was now inside the house.

Lisa sat up and asked, "What happened? Did the creature bring us back here?"

I said, "Yes."

Lisa was in disbelief. Lisa blurts out, "Wow! You stink!"

I laughed and said, "So do you!"

Lisa sniffed her shirt and gagged. We both laughed and Lisa said, "I better get home."

I agreed and said, "We can't tell anyone about this!"

Lisa replied, "For sure! They wouldn't believe us even if we told the truth."

I went inside and took a nice long shower. I hoped that Lisa would do the same!

5

WHAT DO WE DO NOW?

Lisa was feeling much better a couple of days later. After doing my morning chores around the farm I gave Lisa a call. I asked her if she wanted to go back into the woods. This time, Lisa was the one that was a little reluctant, but I convinced her that, if this creature wanted to hurt us, it could have, but it didn't. She agreed and with slight reluctance, Lisa came over.

We met outside by the barn. Lisa asked, "I wonder what they eat?"

I replied, "I'm not sure. Maybe granola bars or apples and bananas." I ran back inside the house and grabbed some snacks to give to the creature so that it would know we meant it no harm.

Snacks for the creature

Lisa and I took a deep breath and headed up the hill toward the woods, and as we got to the top I asked Lisa, "Are you sure this is a good idea?"

Lisa laughed a little and replied, "This is definitely not a good idea!"

I chuckled and said, "I think you might be right!" We looked at each other and I shrugged my shoulders.

Lisa said, "Well we've come this far already. We'll never know unless we try."

I responded, "Hopefully the both of us come out of this alive!"

Lisa smacked my arm and grabbed my hand pulling me toward the woods. She sure has been good at dragging me around.

We walked quietly all the way back to the location where we had encountered the creature last time. We sat on the hillside above the ravine for about an hour with no sight of the creature. Of course, there were the usual suspects; birds, squirrels and chipmunks, scrambling around.

We then decided to make our way to the bottom of the ravine and waded across the small stream to the pines area where we had originally seen the creature. There was no sign of anything unusual until a rock came flying by us out of nowhere. Then another rock came through the trees. Lisa looked at me with fright in her eyes.

I said, "It has to be the creature. No other animal in the woods could possibly throw a rock."

Lisa yelled out, "Hey, it's us again! We mean no harm!" There was no response.

I then remembered how the creature whooped, and I had heard a whoop reply the last time we saw the creature. I mimicked what I had heard. "Whoop!"

Lisa quickly said, "What are you doing?"

I whooped again. "Whoop!"

Then from across the stream we heard a loud whoop! Lisa and I looked at each other with surprise.

I whooped again. "Whoop!"

Then from across the stream we heard another whoop! I'm not

sure what this meant but I felt as though I was actually communi-cating with the creature. I wasn't sure what it meant in their language. I was hopeful that what I was saying was something good or peaceful. I sure didn't want to be disrespectful and have the creature become angry or violent.

Lisa then joined in and whooped as well. Again, another whoop from across the stream. We both laughed a little. Slowly from behind a big tree steps out the creature. It seemed to be a little wary of us.

We waved and Lisa said, "We won't hurt you!" The creature grunted and stepped a little closer. I reached into my backpack and grabbed the snacks we brought. I held them up and threw a few across the stream. The creature just looked at them. I opened a granola bar, took a bite and rubbed my belly. Lisa did the same. The creature reached down and grabbed a granola bar and started to take a bite with the wrapper still on.

We both yelled, "Stop!"

The creature let out a loud grunt and took a step back. I could almost feel that it was startled. I quickly grabbed another granola bar and showed the creature how to open it. The creature was not gentle enough and as it opened the granola bar it broke into pieces, and it all dropped to the ground. The creature inquisitively picked up some off the ground and sniffed the granola bar. The creature looked at me and I motioned for him to put it in his mouth. The creature slowly put it in its mouth and chewed it. The creature grabbed more of the granola bar and ate it.

I yelled out, "He likes it!" I threw him two more that I had in my backpack.

The creature quickly tore them open and ate them. We couldn't believe it! We are feeding a Bigfoot! Lisa took a couple of pictures on her phone.

I said, "We have to be careful that those pictures don't get into the wrong hands." Lisa nodded in agreement. We then heard from deeper in the woods what sounded like a tree knock. The creature quickly replied. However, it used its throat to make the noise. I remembered hearing about gorillas making throat clicks and clucks from a TV show about them. They must be related to gorillas and humans, however, since they truly look like a mix of both. Then there was a return tree knock, or should I say a throat knock, was again heard from deeper in the woods. The creature turned and without hesitation ran very quickly up the other side of the ravine toward where the other throat knocks had come from. The creature was much quicker than any person could ever run up such a steep incline. The creature did it with such ease. Once it got to the top it looked back at us and made a deep, gruff noise. It turned and disappeared over the top of the ridge.

Lisa and I just looked at each other and smiled with excitement. We both just couldn't believe what had just happened to us.

Lisa said, "Jacob, we better get back!"

I agreed and we climbed back up our side of the ravine, taking much longer than it took for the creature to climb. Plus, we were quite winded by the time we reached the top. The first thing that came to my mind was, I wonder how amazing it would be to have an entire football team of these creatures. Even the Professional Football World Champions wouldn't stand a chance against these creatures.

Lisa then stated, "It was weird, I swear that it was talking to us, or I could almost understand what it was thinking."

"Ya, I thought the same thing." I replied. "Maybe it's just wishful thinking?" I added.

"Maybe?" Lisa replied.

Once we returned to the farm, Lisa and I sat down to check out her pictures of the creature. Lisa frantically blurted out, "What the heck?" I looked and I couldn't believe my eyes. We were about fifteen feet away when Lisa took the pictures of the creature, however, they were completely blurry. All you could see was a dark blurry mass. No detail at all! We were so disappointed. We had thought that we had gotten indisputable proof that these creatures actually existed.

Lisa commented, "Maybe what they say about the creatures is true! You know that they have some magnetic aura that interferes with electronics?"

"I had heard that but without proper evidence, who knows for sure?" I replied.

All I knew was that we were going to have to do some research. We need to find out as much as we can before going back. We want to be as prepared as possible next time we encounter this creature. Lisa and I are very determined to get un-refutable proof and evidence that these creatures really do exist.

6

RESEARCH

It was very baffling that the pictures that were taken turned out blurry. We couldn't really explain why. They just got blurrier as we tried to zoom in. All the photos that Lisa had taken before and after those of the creature are all perfectly clear.

Lisa and I started researching information about Bigfoot and Sasquatch on my computer. We found out they have many names throughout the country and actually reports of similar creatures from all around the world. We learned that there have been sightings since the beginning of human existence, it seems. Many native tribes have stories of very large, wild, hairy apelike but still manlike creatures that lived in the woods all over North America. The native tribes described them as spiritual creatures and have intergraded their culture around them. Native tribes also believed they were inter-dimensional beings, meaning they could appear and disappear by moving from one dimension to another dimension. The creatures live in another realm but can bend light to create portals that allow them to travel in and out of our dimension anytime they want. It was also said they come into our dimension to enjoy our world and they don't really want to interact with humans. The only reason that we ever see them is that we surprise them while they are distracted enjoying their favorite areas of our world.

Lisa commented, "That sure would explain why they just seem to disappear and why electronics lose power or that pictures are always blurry."

The information also noted that native lore says that these creatures are not afraid of us in any way and that there is nothing we can ever do to hurt them.

Lisa spoke up and added with a high-pitched voice, "Oh my goodness, Jacob! I can't get over that I was sensing something while we were across the creek from it! I felt like it was talking directly into my brain! I knew it wanted more granola bars. I just didn't want you to think that I was going crazy!"

I interrupted, "Yes, I felt like it was talking to me as well!"

"It wasn't saying anything out loud so that our ears could hear it but literally talking to us inside of our heads." Lisa blurted out, "There're telepathic!"

We both sat there trying to absorb all the information we had been reading. There was so much information and stories as we researched further. So many experiences from other people matched up with what we were experiencing.

We both took a deep breath and continued researching. We then ran across a video from Bluff Creek in the Northern California mountains of a Bigfoot that walked across a stream bed and then off into the hills. The creature in the video looked just like our creature. With so many pictures and videos out there, this is the only one that looked anything like our creature. This is not to say that they might have seen similar creatures.

Lisa then suggested, "Why don't we join some of the social media Bigfoot groups to see if we could gather any information."

I thought that would be a great idea. We noticed on a few of the videos that there was a cryptic researcher that was looking for more information from anyone who had seen Bigfoot.

Lisa asked, "Do we call him?"

I added, "If we do, we are putting ourselves out there to possibly be ridiculed. We have no conclusive evidence that it really exists."

Lisa replied, "You're right. We should wait until we have better evidence. We must go back and get a hair sample to bring to the researcher."

I confirmed, "Great idea, Lisa! Let's plan on going back into the ravine where we saw him this weekend. These creatures must have left behind some sort of evidence that they exist." I added. "My father has to work this Saturday, and we have church Sunday morning. I think Saturday morning after my chores would be best."

Lisa smiled and said, "It's a date then!"

I looked at her thinking to myself, "What is she talking about? That's not a date!"

7

RETURN TO THE RAVINE

It was a beautiful, warm sunny Saturday morning. As soon as my father left for work, I got on the phone and called Lisa. However, Lisa's mother answered the phone and asked, "Hey, Jacob, what are you two kids up to today?"

I was caught a little off guard by her question. I had to come up with something! And quick! I then responded with the truth, "We are going hiking in our woods."

Lisa's mom replied with excitement, "I'm so glad that Lisa has someone to hang out with, Jacob! Make sure you are both careful and be out of those woods by dark."

I replied, "Of course."

Then I could hear Lisa asking her mom in the background, "Is that Jacob?" Lisa's mom then handed Lisa the phone. Lisa asked, "Hey Jacob! Are you ready to go?"

I replied, "Yes, I have a whole box of granola bars too!"

Lisa commented, "That's awesome! I have a couple bottles of juice and ziplock sandwich baggies and tweezers to hopefully get some hair samples!"

I responded, "Great! Hurry up and get here!"

Jacob and Lisa visit the ravine

Lisa came back with, "Aren't you going to come pick me up for our date?"

I just ignored her and said, "Just get here."

As I was hanging up, I could hear Lisa's voice in frustration yell out, "Ahhhhh!"

My mother came into the kitchen and asked the same as Lisa's mom, "What are you up to with Lisa today?"

I told her the same, "We are going for a hike in the woods."

My mother then commented with some sarcasm, "Let's not end up in the hospital again, Jacob!"

I smiled as I was grabbing my backpack and replied, "That was an accident, mother. We will be very careful."

My mother had a look on her face as if she didn't fully believe me.

As I walked out the front door onto our porch, I could see Lisa pulling into the driveway riding her pink bike with a bell, long pink and white tassels hanging from the handlebars. I smiled and chuckled to myself thinking I would never be caught dead on her bike. My bike was a plain flat black primer with a couple glossy black flames on the frame. Much more my style.

As Lisa pulled up next to me, she asks in an angry way, "What are you smiling about?"

I was caught off guard by her attitude and replied, "Just how cute your bike is. That's all!"

Lisa snarled and said, "At least it's not boring and depressing like your bike!"

I thought to myself, what does she know?

As Lisa parked her bike she asked, "Are you ready to go?" She seemed to be upset about something.

I asked her, "Did I do something wrong?"

Lisa, acting very frustrated, responded with, "Jacob! Seriously? You have no clue, do you? I don't want to talk about it! Let's just go!"

Lisa stormed ahead of me toward the trail to the woods. I stood there for a second wondering, what on earth had I done?

The whole way into the woods Lisa never said a word to me. I tried to talk to her several times with no reply. I would even hurry to walk beside her, but Lisa would walk even faster.

I finally stopped and said, "Whatever I did Lisa, I'm very sorry! I never meant to upset you!"

Lisa stopped, snapped around with a look of anger and blurted out, "If you don't like me Jacob, all you have to do is tell me! It's not like we're getting married! I thought we were more than friends and we could call our time together a date! But if you don't want any relationship with me then fine! After we prove that these creatures exist, we can go our separate ways!"

I literally stood there in shock. I had no idea that we were anywhere near being in a relationship. It was the farthest thing from my mind. I like her but I thought that she was cool, for a girl that is. I mean, we are not even 12 years old yet.

I remembered what my father would sometimes say to my mother when she would yell at him. It always made my mother stop yelling and they would hug. Lisa had started walking again. I ran up next to her and said, "You're right! I wasn't thinking. I'm sorry for hurting your feelings."

Lisa again, stopped in her tracks. Her face was beet red with tears in her eyes. I then did what my father would do and gave Lisa a big hug and a kiss on the forehead.

Lisa hugged me tightly and said, "Thank you for apologizing." I could tell she was happy now. She started to smile and said, "I'm still mad at you!"

I smiled because that's exactly how my mother would act after my father apologized.

We both began walking again toward the ravine. This time it was side by side.

As we approached the ravine, Lisa heard something and reached across me with her hand to stop me. We knelt down on the grassy ground of the woods, and she whispered, "I want to get the camera ready so we can get a picture." I nodded in agreement. Once she readied the camera, we crawled to the edge to where we could see the creek down below. We laid there for about twenty minutes, and we saw nothing but squirrels, chipmunks, and more birds.

I whispered, "What if they're not around?"

Lisa shrugged and whispered back, "They have to be around." Lisa rolled over on her back and gasped.

I said, "Shhhh!"

Lisa interrupted and said, "Jacob, what is that?"

I looked up to see what she was talking about. The tree cover was very dense, but I finally saw what she was now pointing at. In total dismay I said, "Whoa! What is that?"

Lisa shook her head and said, "It looks like a mirage."

There was a big spot in the trees that looked like something I had seen in an alien movie. The area was all wavy compared to the surrounding area. Lisa grabbed the camera and started taking pictures. We were both in awe.

I said, "Maybe it's a gateway to another realm or world." I reached over the edge of the ravine and grabbed a loose rock.

Lisa asked, "What are you doing?"

I replied, "I want to see what happens when I throw a rock into it." I stood up and nervously launched the rock into the mirage. As the rock went into the mirage, the mirage wiggled like a bowl of jello, the rock disappeared and then nothing.

Lisa commented, "The rock didn't fall after it went through the mirage. That would mean that it went somewhere. Right?"

I thought for a second and replied, "It isn't here, so it had to have gone somewhere else. But where?"

Lisa said, "Do it again! Throw another rock into it!"

I reached over the edge and grabbed a bigger rock. I stood, reared my back, and launched it into the mirage. Again, the mirage wiggled, and the rock disappeared.

"Where are these rocks going, Jacob?" Lisa asked.

I replied with disbelief, "I have no clue. Maybe another world or dimension like we read online."

Lisa and I had come up here to prove that these giant creatures existed and now we are trying to figure out another completely baffling mystery. This defies all logic and I'm not sure if I really want to find out what this is. What if it's dangerous? What if it's connected to the creature? All these questions were running through both our minds as we just kept gazing up at it.

Suddenly we heard something down below at the bottom of the ravine. We rolled back over to see what it was. We couldn't see anything.

Lisa whispered, "I hear it talking into my head."

I asked, "What's it saying?" As soon as Lisa started to speak, I stopped her by grabbing her hand. I replied quickly with, "I hear it too! It knows we are up here and to stay where we are."

Lisa asked, "How can we understand it? It's speaking to us, but we don't hear anything, but we know what it's saying!"

I shrugged and before you knew it the creature was standing about ten feet away. It had climbed the side of the ravine in mere seconds. The creature was big, hairy, and muscular, at least eight to nine feet tall with really long arms. It looked like an ape and a human mixed together. It had no sort of clothing. It was like looking at a wild animal but intelligent like a human. The eyes were an orangey color. When it looked at you it was like it was looking right into your brain. Lisa looked up at the mirage in the trees and pointed at it. I could actually hear in my brain when Lisa asked the creature, "What is that?"

The creature replied without speaking, "That is our doorway between your world and ours."

The creature knew exactly what I was thinking at that moment, "Can we see your world?"

The creature answered with, "No, it is very dangerous for humans to enter our world." The creature continued with, "Humans have accidentally entered our world through open doorways and found themselves without protection from other creatures in our world that are very dangerous and would not hesitate to protect their territory."

I asked without speaking to the creature, "What do we call you?"

The creature responded, "We are known as Sastach's. We are the supreme beings in our world." The creature and I then could tell that Lisa had a question.

Lisa was asking, "Why do you come here to our world?"

The creature responded, "Because we are able to, first of all, but also because our world does not have large plant life due to a different atmosphere. So, we can enjoy the great wooded lands around your world."

I then asked, again without speaking a word, "What do we call you?"

The creature stood up really tall and introduced itself as Rompada.

Lisa then asked the creature, "Are we the first humans that your kind have spoken to?"

"No," the creature replied, "We have been speaking to chosen humans since the beginning of time."

Lisa asked another question, "Why did you choose to talk to us?"

The creature answered, "You both surprised me and I needed to be close enough to read your minds to tell if you can be of the "trusted ones". You both have pure spirits and can be trusted by our kind."

I asked, "How many of you come here?"

The creature replied, "Nearly all of the Sastach's are able to bend light to be able to exist into your world, but most do not. The ones that do not are afraid of humans and their intentions." The creature added, "Even though humans can do no harm to us, many see humans as evil creatures that do not respect or cherish their world."

Lisa replied to the creature, "I see what you mean but not all of us are bad."

The creature said, "One last thing...we know that humans want to prove our existence but in reality, we exist only on our world and can only visit here. We must leave after only a short time before our existence fades in our natural world. Meaning we would cease to exist. That is why I must go now! Remember, for us to be able to see each other in the future we must be able to trust you not to reveal our secrets." The creature then walked toward the doorway back to his world and leapt into it without hesitation and disappeared.

The doorway, or portal as some would call it, was now gone as well.

8

KEEPING THE SECRET

As Lisa and I walked back home, we talked about everything that had just happened. We were excited about seeing our creature friend, which has a name now. Also, all the new and wild science fiction possibilities of interdimensional travel between different worlds. On the other hand, we were somewhat defeated that we couldn't mention a word of any of these experiences to anyone. Who would believe us anyway?

Once we got back down to the house, Lisa and I sat on a swing on the front porch of our farmhouse.

Lisa then asked me, "How were we able to hear each other's thoughts?"

I replied, "I'm not sure but it sure was strange to communicate without speaking aloud."

"Yes, I almost felt like you and I had the same brain," replied Lisa.

I then thought it would be cool to see if Lisa could still read my thoughts, even though I really didn't want her to know what I was always thinking about. I asked Lisa, "Hey, let's do a little test. What am I thinking about now?" I had a predetermined thing I was thinking of, that she would not know unless I told her.

Lisa looked at me and smiled and blurted out, "Food! Jacob!" I was astounded that she could still read my mind yet, I couldn't tell what she was thinking. She then laughed, "You are so easy."

I asked, "What do you mean?"

Lisa replied, "You're always thinking of food!" We both got a laugh.

I felt relieved actually, that she could no longer read my mind. Strangely enough, I've caught myself looking at her as more than just a friend. She is very pretty with her long brown hair, brown eyes and nice smile. She always makes me feel like I'm the only person in the world. Even at school she tends to snarl at other boys and always wants to be near me. I must have been smiling while I was running all of this through my mind because Lisa was calling out my name.

"Jacob, what on earth are you smiling about?"

I quickly responded with, "Nothing!" Lisa had the look of *I don't believe you* on her face. So, I added, "I was thinking about you!"

Lisa laughed and said, "I highly doubt that, Jacob!"

Lisa started to walk away, and I blurted out, "Don't go! Stay for dinner. I'm sure my parents wouldn't mind."

Lisa answered, "I'll have to check with my parents." Lisa called, talked to her mom, and was able to talk her parents into it."

I said to Lisa, "Yes! Awesome! Then it's a date!"

Lisa looked at me shaking her head with slight frustration and sighed. As she walked by me toward the house she uttered, "It's not a date!"

Now, I felt how Lisa did when I said that to her. I guess I deserved that. I knew deep down inside that she didn't mean it though.

My mother had already set a plate for Lisa as we sat down at the table. My mother even gave up her spot of sitting next to me to allow Lisa to sit there. My mother seemed to be pushing the cute narrative of Lisa and I being together. I felt that although it's nice sharing time with Lisa, I have a long life ahead of me. I mean, what's the rush?

As we ate, my father asked, "What have you two been up to today?"

I replied, "Not much, just went hiking in the woods."

My father caught us off guard with his next question. "Did you see any monsters this time?"

Lisa and I looked at each other with fear of being caught. I answered with a chuckle, "Not this time!"

Lisa's eyes bugged out and she added with her own giggle, "No monsters, just a time traveling wormhole!"

Both my parents laughed out loud. My mom added, "You two really like to goof around. Such wild imaginations you kids have."

Once again, Lisa had answered with the truth. I was a little in shock by her answer but then thought that as long as we keep our secrets to ourselves, we can continue to see the creature and learn more about him. We both have so many questions to ask the creature.

After dinner Lisa and I made a long, well-thought-out list of all the questions we could possibly think of asking the creature. We both felt kind of special that we were interacting with something that most people don't believe even exists. I guess it would compare to being an astronaut and visiting an exciting new world and finding intelligent life. Both our thoughts raced as we imagined all the possibilities.

My mother called up to us and said, "It's time to get Lisa back home, Jacob."

"Ok!" I hollered back. We jumped into the truck and headed toward Lisa's house.

As we drove around the corner my mother suddenly slammed on the breaks and yelled out, "What was that?" Something large had darted across the road in front of the truck. My mother thought she might have hit it. She said, "You two stay into the truck. I'm going to check to see if I can figure out what that might have been." We know that an injured animal can be dangerous.

As she opens the door I said, "Be careful mother!"

As she slowly opened the door and stepped out of the truck, we could smell something terrible. Lisa hit my arm and quietly said, "It smells like the creature, Jacob."

"It does!" I replied.

As my mother cautiously rounded the front of the truck, she stopped dead in her tracks. Her mouth was wide open and eyes bulging out as she looked at something. She bent over and picked something up. As she came back to her door, we could see that she was holding something in her arms. She climbed back into the truck, turned, smiled at us and said, "Looks like monsters are real!" Lisa and I were completely puzzled. What did she have? My mother then laughed and handed a big fluffy rabbit to me. "Now you have a new pet, Jacob!" The rabbit didn't seem injured at all. My mother commented, "Not nearly as big as what I thought I saw!" She added, "Let's get Lisa home."

"Ya, let's." I replied. Lisa and I just looked at each other and exhaled in relief that it wasn't the creature, however what she almost hit had to have been the creature.

9

TORNADO

Tonight, I was suddenly awakened to the voice of my father yelling, "Get up Jacob! There's a Tornado heading our way!"

I jumped up immediately and ran downstairs to the hallway outside my parents' bedroom where my parents were.

The whole house was shaking and there was a terrible crashing sound coming from outside. The windows were rattling from the incredible wind that was blowing. My mother grabbed my hand as my father pulled us toward the back door that was near the cellar under the house. The noise was frightening and so loud that it sounded like a freight train going right through the house. I could barely hear my father say, "We have to get to the cellar now!"

As we opened the back door, we couldn't see a thing. All the lights were out. The volume outside was even louder with large debris crashing all around. My father guided us to the cellar door. He struggled to pull the door open and then keep it open long enough for us all to get down the stairs. Once my mother and I were inside the cellar he pulled the doors closed and grabbed a lantern he had stored for such emergencies. The house was literally shaking above us. I could feel dust falling onto us from above. Just as my father was able to get the lantern lit, the storm was already passing. The noise outside started to subside and become less and sound further away.

My father said, "I think I'm going to check outside. You two stay here until I get back."

Jacob's house after the tornado

I could feel my mother was trembling as she held onto me and said, "Be careful!"

My father slowly opened the cellar door and peered outside. It was still pitch black out. He took the lantern he had lit so we followed behind my father as he walked outside. As we reached the top of the stairs, we could still hear the tornado tearing through the trees of our woods. There were loud snaps of trees breaking and the howl of the wind. Then suddenly it was now dead quiet around the farm.

The tornado had gone as quickly as it had come. My father looked at us and asked, "Are you both alright?"

My mother replied, "I'm good! How about you, Jacob?"

I answered back, "I'm Okay!"

My father then held the lantern up as high as he could. He turns around and commented, "It seems the house is still all there." We walked around toward the front of the house to access the damage. "It doesn't look too bad. Just a little banged up." My father stated with relief.

The farmyard light turned back on and then we could see that the barn was heavily damaged. We quickly walked toward the barn through all the debris that had been strewn everywhere.

My mother commented, "I sure hope all the animals are ok!"

My father and I grabbed some loose boards that had piled up in front of the barn doors and threw them aside. We could hear that the horses were quite riled inside. We then pried open the doors to find that all the animals were good. Just a little riled up. My mother and I quickly calmed down the horses by petting and talking softly to them.

My father gave a big, "Phew! We are lucky not to have that much damage!"

My mother responded, "I hope it didn't hit any other farms."

Right then I thought about Lisa and her family. I asked, "Can we go check on Lisa and her family? Please?"

My father said, "Yes, good idea." My father ran in and grabbed his keys and told us to get on the tractor.

My mother questions, "The tractor?"

My father replied, "Yes, in case there are trees down in the road."

I knew how to grab the chainsaw and supplies. My father backed the tractor up and hooked up the old hay wagon. I piled the chainsaw, gas, and oil onto the trailer.

My dad asked, "Are we all ready to go?"

My mother and I, without saying a word, climbed aboard the hay wagon with slight trepidation of not knowing what we may find down the road, and had me feeling anxious. All I knew was we had to get to Lisa and her family ASAP!

We didn't get far before we ran across trees downed over the road. My mother kept the work light on the tractor, pointing in our direction as we worked. My father reminded me not to cut completely through the tree so to not hit the chainsaw blade onto the road or ground. That would dull the teeth on the chain rapidly. Even in an emergency situation, my father was teaching me how to do things the right way.

My father was big on taking care of your tools, so you have them ready when you need them. This is an emergency, and he could never have been more right.

We cleared several trees before being able to move ahead. As we moved closer to Lisa's house, we could hear chainsaws and see lights coming from that direction on the road. Finally, we reached an area where there were no trees and just open fields. We pulled up out front of Lisa's house and could only see her mom and dad cutting a very large oak tree that had fallen across the roadway.

I jumped out and her mom asked, "Are you all ok?"

My mother replied "Yes, and you guys? Where's Lisa?"

Lisa's mother took a deep breath as she put her shaking hand over her mouth, trying not to cry. Suddenly, from behind the very large rootball of these downed oak trees, emerged Lisa with tears in her eyes. She had been looking for her dog when we pulled up.

She yelled out as she ran closer and hugged me, "Jacob! Oh my god, Jacob! You're ok!" I don't think I've ever been hugged so tightly.

Lisa's dad asked, "How's your house and buildings?"

My dad replied, "A little banged up but repairable." Just as my father started to ask about theirs, my mother pointed the big work light on our tractor towards their house. We all gasped. Their house was almost all gone.

Lisa's dad spoke with a crackle in his voice, "We took a direct hit."

My parents both embraced Lisa's parents as they all started to cry.

Lisa's dad was able to get out, "I guess we're lucky. We are all alive."

Lisa was still holding onto me tightly. She asked me quietly, "Jacob, what are we going to do? We have nowhere to live."

I quickly blurted out, "Couldn't they stay with us? We have that extra room and Lisa could stay in my room. I will gladly sleep on the couch!"

Lisa's dad replied, "We couldn't put you all out like that."

My mother replied, "Nonsense! It's done. You'll stay with us until you get your home back."

"It could take quite a while," replied Lisa's dad.

My mother said, "It's what neighbors do for each other in times of need. I'm sure you would do the same for us." Lisa's parents nodded, still with tears in their eyes.

My father said, "It's settled, climb aboard. We'll come back in the morning to salvage what we can."

Jacob and his new bed, the couch

Everyone climbed aboard the hay wagon and returned to our house.

Once we got back, I showed Lisa to my room and made sure she had everything she needed. Lisa for once was very quiet and seemed in shock.

I asked, "Do you want to talk about anything?"

Lisa just shook her head, laid down and stared at the ceiling.

I softly said, "Okay, I'll be downstairs on the couch if you need anything." Still nothing. I grabbed my sleeping bag out of the closet and started to walk out the door. As I said, "Goodnight," I turned off the light and closed the door.

I got about halfway out the door when I hear Lisa say, "Please leave the door open, Jacob!"

I smiled and said, "No problem."

My parents were just about done setting up the guest room for Lisa's parents when I reached the couch. My parents both said good night and headed for bed. I could hear them say goodnight to Lisa as they walked by. I was beat and with everything that happened tonight, this was the first time in quite a while that I hadn't thought about the creature.

10

MORE TROUBLE

It sure is different waking up to new roommates. Our parents have been up rustling since around five am. I didn't get nearly as much sleep with the loss of my bedroom to Lisa. The couch was fine, but I suddenly had no privacy. Don't get me wrong, I am willing to sacrifice anything for Lisa and her parents.

My mother then yelled out, "Time to eat, kids!" Even though I was still dead tired, I jumped up with new excitement.

After washing up for breakfast, I could see Lisa slowly walking down the stairs. She was not her usual self. I got up and pulled out her chair from the table. I leaned over and asked, "Are you ok?"

Lisa looked at me with a painful look in her eyes and shook her head, "No."

I was now concerned and asked Lisa's parents if she was hurt in the tornado.

"Not that I know of," replied her mother as she got up to take a closer look at Lisa. Her mother asked Lisa, "Are you okay sweetheart?"

With her head down and her eyes closed, she slowly shook her head, "No." Lisa sputtered out painfully, "M, my, my head really hurts."

All of our parents agreed that she may have been hit in the head with some flying debris during the tornado. Lisa's mom grabbed her purse and said, "I'm running her to the hospital."

My mother and I both said, "I'm coming with!" We packed up the truck and rushed Lisa to the hospital.

Once at the hospital we had to wait for an hour before we were able to hear from the doctor. The doctor approached us in the waiting room and said with a very serious tone in her voice, "Lisa has a serious concussion but should make a full recovery." The doctor added, "We've given her something for the pain and something to help her rest."

Lisa's mother asked, "Could we see her now?"

"You'll have to wait a bit. Give us some time to get her admitted and put her into a room. Maybe, get something to eat down at the cafeteria."

Lisa's dad nervously asked, "It's that serious that she has to stay overnight?"

The doctor answered, "Yes, we have to take more ex-rays to make sure she didn't suffer any other injuries. I'll have my assistant stop down for you to sign some papers. Once we read the ex-rays we'll know more. Lisa is in good hands. We'll take good care of her." The doctor then turned and walked away.

We all headed to the cafeteria for some lunch. Once we all sat down, Lisa's mom commented with a slight anger in her voice, "We haven't even had time to think about our home being gone and now our only child is in the hospital. What's next?"

Lisa's dad optimistically replied, "We can't think like that. We have a long road ahead, but I promise that everything is going to be all right!"

As we were eating our lunch the insurance agent called Lisa's dad to go over the damage of their home. After several minutes of discussion, Lisa's dad announced with a smile, "I told you everything was going to be fine! The insurance company will be rebuilding our home. We can rebuild it the same or have a completely modern design."

Lisa's mom smiled, "So I finally get the kitchen I've always wanted? A bathroom and walk-in closet I desperately need?"

Lisa's dad laughed and said, "Within reason! We can build up to the value of the old house! Maybe a little more." He added toward Lisa's mom, "We will have to go over plans with a home builder. You can let them know what your desires are, and we'll try our best to fit them in."

This was great news for them. With all the tragedy, they finally had something to look forward to. Now we could only wait to find out about Lisa. I walked off to have some alone time to process everything that was going on. I was so worried about Lisa. I found a quiet spot outside in a courtyard with a large oak tree in the center and a fountain. I sat there thinking of how important Lisa was to me.

As I thought back to all the adventures we've had over the summer so far, all I could do is appreciate what a great friend she has always been. I was shocked as I started to tear up a little. I've never felt like this about anyone before. I wasn't sure how to feel about my feelings about Lisa. All I knew was she had to get better so she could continue to be part of my life. I reached into my pocket and pulled out a coin. I held it tightly in my hand and made a wish that Lisa would be all better. I tossed the coin into the fountain and watched it sway back and forth under the water until it hit the bottom.

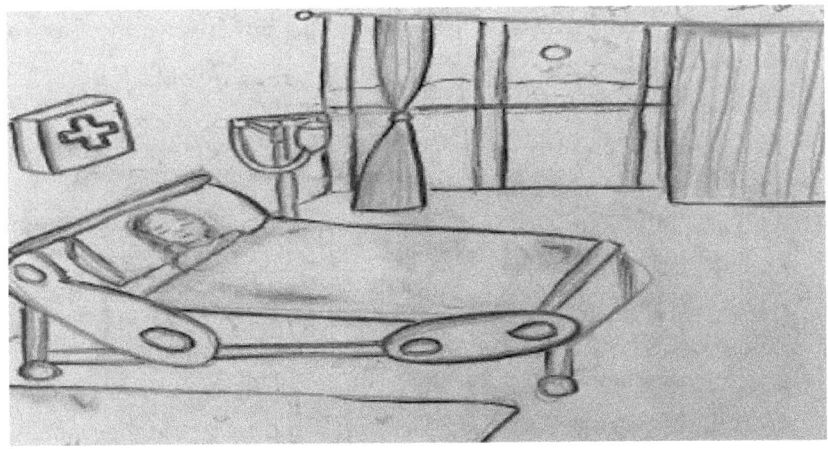

Lisa in the hospital

Just then, my mother stepped out the hospital door and yelled, "Jacob, we can go see Lisa now!"

I sprung up and ran into the cafeteria where they were all waiting for me. We all briskly walked to the elevators. The elevator felt like an eternity to get to Lisa's floor, even though it took only seconds.

I noticed Lisa's mom and dad were holding hands as we entered her room. I could tell they were nervous but excited to be able to see Lisa. As we walked in, Lisa looked at everyone and with some discomfort, smiled. Everyone started tearing up as we took turns hugging her. Of course, I was last, but she seemed to smile a little more as I hugged her.

Lisa quietly said, "I'm surprised you're here, Jacob."

"Where else would I be, silly!" I replied.

Lisa's parents held her hand as they told her the good news about the house.

Lisa opened her eyes wide and excitedly asked, "So I get a new room and my own bathroom now?"

Her parents laughed. "We'll see," replied her dad. It was good to see her feeling better and that my wish was coming true.

The doctor then entered the room to go over Lisa's health. He had nothing but good news. Lisa's concussion was improving, and no other injuries were detected. The doctor just wanted her to stay another day for observation.

My mother came over to me and asked, "Do you want to stay a while longer? I can go home for a bit and come back to get you."

"Sure, that would be awesome!"

Lisa's parents and my mom said goodbye and went home to start conquering all the issues that lie ahead of them.

Lisa smiled and asked, "Are you sure you don't have better things to do than stay here with me, Jacob?"

"This is where I want to be," I answered.

Lisa reached out her hand and said, "Grab a chair and sit by me, please."

I sat down next to her as she held my hand tightly. It made me a little uneasy and wasn't sure what I was feeling. I could tell that she was comfortable holding my hand.

I relaxed a little when she said, "Thanks for coming and staying with me. There's no one I would rather spend my day with!"

I told her, "You should get some rest like the doctor ordered."

Still holding my hand, she nodded her head as she closed her eyes and fell asleep.

With little sleep last night for myself, I fell asleep as well.

11

AFTER THE STORM

Lisa was now home from the hospital and feeling much better. We spent the first few days searching through the rubble of her old house looking for anything salvageable. The bulldozers and removal crew were coming soon to get rid of all the debris in order to clear the way to build the new house. We put anything worth saving in an enclosed trailer for safekeeping. It was a sad time but also a sense of excitement was in the air. Lisa's dad was great at keeping Lisa and her mom's minds positive with thoughts of the new house with the amenities they longed for.

Lisa's dad wanted nothing added for himself in their new house. He just wanted Lisa and her mom to be happy. You could tell that making Lisa and her mom happy is what makes him happy. I feel like I even learned something wonderful about the act of giving from such a terrible situation. I can now see that giving is just as awesome as receiving a gift.

Now that we had the area around the home scoured, Lisa's dad asked me if I could help him search the woods across the street for any belongings that the tornado may have blown over there. We grabbed a couple empty boxes and started picking up all the debris we found littered throughout the woods. There were all sorts of their belongings strewn everywhere. There is even clothing and parts of their house hanging in the trees. I also couldn't believe how many trees were blown down on the path of destruction that the tornado had taken. Luckily for our family, the tornado that had been heading straight for our house changed direction right before it reached the farmstead. I kept thinking how lucky we were to only have minor damage that we could fix on our own. As I kept observing the path of the tornado, it finally struck me...What about our creature friend? Was he okay? Was he here when the tornado struck or was, he in his own dimension? This was the first time I had a chance to think about the creature with everything that was going on. Not even Lisa mentioned anything. I knew once we have a chance, that Lisa and I'll have to go check to make sure that he was okay.

As I kept on picking up debris, I found an old picture lying under one of the fallen trees. The picture was of Lisa's parents, both with big smiles on their faces and two babies. One in each of their arms. I wanted to ask Lisa's dad about it, but he was quite a bit away from me at the moment, so I put the picture in my pocket for now. Lisa's dad and I had filled several trash bags and boxes of debris by the time we were done and headed back to their place. Once we put all the debris into a small shed that wasn't damaged too bad by the tornado, I remembered to ask about the picture that I had found when Lisa's dad receives a call interrupting my question. Once Lisa's dad was off his phone, he asked me if I could sit down for a moment.

He started out with, "Jacob, I want to thank you for all your help. It's much appreciated!"

"No problem." I replied.

He continued, "You're a good boy and a good friend to Lisa. Lisa's mom and I are grateful that she has a friend like you that she can spend quality time with. Especially since, like yourself, she is an only child."

I nodded my head and replied, "I really like hanging out with her, sir! Lisa isn't like all the other girls, and we have lots in common."

Lisa's dad added, "We also appreciate you and your parents taking us into your home until we get ours rebuilt. It can't be easy having strangers in your home."

I replied, "I know I would like to have you all there every day. It's like suddenly our family doubled." I added, "I also can tell that my parents are actually enjoying your company. Even I haven't heard them laugh so much."

He replied, "Well, thank you, Jacob. I'm seeing the same with our family. Sometimes remarkable things can come from tragedy." Lisa's dad laughed as he patted me on the back, ruffled my hair and added, "Except when I'm kicking everyone's butt in Monopoly!" We both laughed out loud. He sure did kick our butts in Monopoly last night. Playing a game really helped everyone relax and take our minds off all the tragedy that has been happening lately.

I quickly forgot about the picture I had found. Plus, I thought the baby belonged to another family member or perhaps a friend of theirs since Lisa's dad had said that Lisa was also an only child. So, I really didn't think too much about it.

Lisa's dad and I joined Lisa and her mom and finished picking up more debris around their farmstead and then we packed it all into the shed with the rest of their possessions, including that picture I had found. I then pulled Lisa aside to talk. I told her my thoughts of our creature friend.

She agreed and said, "We have to get up there to see if he's okay." I nodded in agreement. "Let's go tomorrow morning, right away!" She added.

"Are you sure that you're up for a hike that deep into the woods already?" I asked.

"Of course, Jacob! You worry too much!" Lisa blurted out.

"Okay then. We'll head out right after breakfast and we get all the chores done," I replied.

12

BACK TO THE RAVINE

This morning, I woke up to someone grabbing my arm and almost shaking me off the couch. I opened my eyes to Lisa's smiling face saying, "Get up! Come on sleepy head. We've got places to go and a creature to find!"

I quickly shushed her and said, "Quiet! You'll let our parents know what we're doing!"

Lisa replied with a laugh, "Don't be silly! They've all left to meet the builders at my place. Your breakfast is on the table. Made by yours truly!" Lisa grabbed my hand and pulled me off the couch and escorted me to the table. Sure enough! Breakfast was all ready to eat. A bowl of granola cereal! I sort of chuckled under my breath. Lisa laughed and commented, "You didn't think I had actually made you a real breakfast, did you?" Now hurry up. We got to get going!" Lisa added. I just smiled and ate it as quickly as possible.

Lisa had no idea that my mother had been trying to get me to eat granola cereal for a long time. It just sounded too healthy for me, so I have never tried it. What do you know, I actually liked it! I was about to take my last bite when Lisa grabbed the bowl and headed for the sink with it.

I yelled out, "Hey! I wasn't done with that!"

As Lisa rinsed out the bowl and left it in the sink she yelled out, "Too bad, now let's go!"

I said, "I have to feed and water the animals before we can go."

Lisa replied, "Nope! All done already by both our dads before they left." As I put my shoes on, Lisa proceeded to list off the supplies, she had packed for our hike back to the ravine, "Water bottles, granola bars, bandages, etc."

"Bandages?" I blurted out.

Lisa looked at me with the look of, "Really?"

After thinking about it, I laughed and said, "Good call!"

We both grabbed our backpacks and headed out the door. It was a bright sunny but quiet morning. Lisa is obviously feeling better since she was twenty steps ahead of me already.

I yelled as I raced to catch up, "Wait up!"

Lisa looked back, smiled, and yelled out, "Hurry up slow poke!"

I was now finding out that Lisa is a little competitive. We both then raced up the hill toward the woods.

Once we reached the top, we stopped in our tracks in shock at what we saw. There was a fifty-yard swath of trees that were flattened by the tornado. Some of the trees were even torn right out of the ground, roots, and all! It was as if the tornado had parted the woods like a person would part their hair. The trees on the left side are all facing the left too and the trees on the right are all facing the right.

I commented to Lisa, "I guess my dad and I'll have plenty of wood to cut for winter."

Lisa stated as we surveyed all the damage, "Let's keep going."

After a long hike we finally approached the ravine. This time we weren't sneaking up or trying to be quiet. We were on a mission to see the creature and make sure he was okay. As we searched the area down below, everything seemed pretty normal. You could see birds flying around, and squirrels in the trees, leaping from branch to branch. Even a deer was drinking from the creek that ran through the bottom of the ravine.

Lisa then suggested, "Let's look for the portal that we had seen before."

I agreed and headed over to the spot we had seen it previously. We looked but saw nothing. "What if we lay down like when you noticed it last time?" I asked. We both laid down on our backs and again, saw nothing.

"What if, the creature won't come back?" Lisa asked. "Maybe it felt like we would ruin its experience of enjoying this area?" Lisa added.

I replied, "Maybe! Maybe, it likes to be left alone like other forest animals. You don't see deer or squirrels running up to us, do you?"

Lisa paused with thought and replied, "I guess you're right! Maybe it just wants to be left alone to enjoy its time visiting our world." We both sat up and looked over the area again. Still no sign of our friend, the creature. Lisa reluctantly said, "What a waste of time!"

I thought for a second and said, "I have an idea. Let's leave the granola bars here on this big tree so that it knows we were here looking for him."

Lisa smiled and said, "That's a great idea Jacob! A sort of way to communicate with him." We put the granola bars in a clear sandwich bag and set them as high as we could in the crook of the branch, easily visible with a piece of reflective tape on the bag. Lisa commented as we admired our work, "The creature can't miss seeing that!" We packed up our things and started heading home.

Lisa was back to being her bubbly self after seeing that the creature was most likely okay. I was also glad to see that she had fully recovered from her concussion. She had us all very worried.

As we were walking back, we crossed into the swath of downed trees from the tornado. This reminded me of the old photo that I had found of her parents holding two babies. Not thinking too much about it I asked, "Hey, while cleaning up debris in the woods with your dad, by your house, I found a picture of your parents with two babies. I figured one was you but who's the other baby?"

Lisa looked at me and with a serious tone to her voice and said, "Sit down Jacob," as she pointed at one of the fallen trees by which we were walking.

I was a little caught off guard, but I followed her direction and sat on the downed tree.

Lisa took a deep breath and blew it out slowly.

I was beginning to think I asked a question that she wasn't prepared to answer. I quickly stated, "No big deal. I don't need to know."

Lisa responded, "No, it's fine. It's just a sensitive subject." I didn't know what to think. What could be so emotional in that picture? Lisa took another deep breath and answered, "Jacob, that other baby was my twin brother, Alex. He only lived a couple weeks after we were born." I stood up and hugged Lisa. Lisa then continued as we hugged, with tears running down her face. "Alex had lung problems and came down with Pneumonia. The doctors did everything they could but to no avail."

I held Lisa tightly and said, "I'm so sorry about your twin brother, Alex. I'm also sorry for bringing it up. I had no idea."

"It's ok, Jacob, you couldn't have known." Lisa replied. We looked at each other and Lisa smiled. She then said, "He's looking down on us now. I'm sure of it!"

I added, "I'm sure he is." Then with my, slightly off brand of humor, "Maybe he knows about our friend and can put in a good word for us!"

Lisa laughed and said, "I have an idea and with your permission, I would like to name the creature after my brother Alex."

My mouth dropped open in shock. "Yes! That would be awesome!" I replied.

Lisa responded, "That will make it easy to talk about the creature, I mean Alex, without our parents catching on."

I added, "Ya, great idea! I just hope the creature doesn't mind!" We both laughed and headed for home.

The whole way back I was thinking about the fact that not only was the farm my home, but it was now Lisa's and her family's home.

Once again Lisa looked at me and asked, "What on earth are you smiling about, Jacob?"

I just continued to smile and replied, "Nothing, nothing at all."

13

LONG NIGHT

The very first thing I wanted to do before I went to bed was to make sure that Lisa wasn't making my breakfast. So, I stated to my mother, "Please tell me that you're going to be around to make breakfast tomorrow morning!"

My mother laughed and asked, "What? Don't you like Lisa's cooking?"

"Cooking?" I asked. "All she made me was granola cereal!"

My mother smiled and said, "Well, since they will be staying with us for a while, I guess I'll have to teach her how to cook then. So, yes, I will be making breakfast in the morning." She added.

I commented with relief. "Thank goodness!"

My mother then asked, "Why don't you help me?"

I was surprised by her request but nodded and told her, "Sure! I would love to. Just wake me up!" I was kind of eager to learn how to cook my own breakfast much less cook for others. I knew I couldn't do any worse than Lisa. Lisa's idea of making breakfast had no cooking involved. I thought it would be nice to help out. Just then, Lisa came strolling down the stairs. I asked, "What's up? Do you need something?"

She shook her head, "No." Then added, "I just have a lot on my mind."

"Like what?" I asked as I made room for her to sit by me on the couch.

"Well, for starters, I feel bad for taking your room and you having to sleep here on this old, beat up, lumpy couch!"

I laughed and replied, "Hey, I happen to like this old, beat up, lumpy couch."

Lisa continued, "I like that I'm getting a new room with my own bathroom, but I also miss my old room and all my things that were destroyed in the tornado."

I could feel the conflict that plagued Lisa. I almost felt like I had when "Alex" (our creature friend) had allowed us to communicate telepathically. I could feel Lisa's feelings. Then, I asked myself, "Or are they my own feelings? I couldn't tell. This telepathy way of communicating is all new to us. I reached out with open arms to Lisa and said, "I'm so sorry Lisa. We will make lots of new memories together. Now come give me a hug."

Lisa hugged me tightly and replied, "Yes, we will! You're so sweet, Jacob. I'm glad we have each other." Lisa added.

We continued talking for a few hours about everything under the sun before we both finally fell asleep.

I was in the deepest sleep and hearing my name being called. "Jacob! Jacob, sweetie! Let's get up sleepy head!" It was my mother. I slowly opened my eyes. It was still dark out. I shook off how sleepy I was and sat up to find Lisa sleeping on the floor next to me. She hadn't slept in my room. I stepped over to her quietly and headed to the kitchen.

My mother put her arm around me and asked, "Are you ready for this?"

I shook my head yes and listened to all my mother's directions. After about forty-five minutes, we had prepared the feast for everyone.

We had coffee, eggs, bacon, biscuits, sausage gravy and my favorite, waffles!

Jacob cooking breakfast

My mother then yelled out, "Breakfast is ready! Come and get it!"

My father and Lisa's parents made their way to the table. I walked into the living room to find Lisa folding her blanket.

I announced, "I made breakfast for you!"

Lisa said with disbelief as we headed to the table, "Ya, sure you did!"

My mother interrupted, "It's true! Jacob did make breakfast for everyone!"

Lisa's parents commented, "Wow!"

My father added with surprise, "Ya, wow!"

I felt super proud that I had helped my mother but also it felt really good that I did something for Lisa and her parents. I wanted them to like me. Throughout breakfast, there was nothing but compliments from everyone. I now have a much larger appreciation for how much work goes into making meals three times a day, from my mother. Now it's time to get to my morning chores!

14

WHAT WAS THAT?

A new morning has come to the farm. The distraction of my head injury this summer and all the work related to the tornado combined with all the repairs needed around our farm has us really unprepared for the harvest this fall. Not to mention, all the firewood needed before the harsh winter starts. If we don't get enough wood cut by the time heavy snow starts, we will be in for a very long, frigid winter. We won't be able to climb the trail leading up the big hill into the woods. Not even with the tractor. Being a Saturday, my father wanted the two of us to get an early start on the morning farm chores and then head into the woods to start cutting up all those trees that had been blown down by the tornado.

We quickly ate our breakfast before heading out to do the chores. We could hear from outside the barn Lisa's dad calling for us.

My father yelled out, "We're in the barn."

Lisa's dad smiled and asked, "I would love to help you two cut some firewood today."

Then we heard Lisa add, "Me too!"

My father replied, "Great, we can use all the help we can get!"

All together we finished the chores quickly and loaded the truck with all the chainsaws, axes, gas, and oil. My father drove the tractor with the wagon, while Lisa's dad drove our farm truck. We all headed up the hill into the woods.

As we approached the top of the hill, Lisa's dad commented, "Oh my goodness!" as he surveyed the land of all the downed trees and destruction from the tornado.

My father found a good place to start cutting the trees up and parked the tractor as close as he could to make it easier to load the trailer. We pulled up next to him with the truck, all jumped out with anticipation, and started grabbing all the tools to get started.

My father made the comment, "Well, at least we don't have to worry about cutting these trees down first. Mother Nature sure has taken care of that for us!"

We didn't like cutting down live trees. It was more dangerous and a live or standing tree took some planning for safety. We always had to predict what way we wanted it to fall. If a person were careless, they could get hurt or even worse.

My father made up a plan of what all our jobs were going to be. Lisa's dad and my father were going to trim branches and cut the trees into one-foot slices. Lisa and I had the responsibility of piling up the branches as they cut them off. Then we would load the cut logs onto the back of the truck and trailer. The larger pieces that we couldn't lift would need to be split before loading.

Things sure happened faster with the help of Lisa and her dad. We were able to take two loads of wood down to the house before our moms even brought us lunch. We grabbed a log chair for everyone to sit in a circle. Then a large one in the center to set up the food.

Lisa's mom made the best meatloaf sandwiches I've ever had, though it could have been that we all worked really hard all morning and were super hungry. It was like going camping and we were having a family picnic.

Everyone was chatting and laughing. Lisa's mom commented, "It's so peaceful up here. I could sit up here every day." She added, "I sure can see why you kids like it up here so much."

Our lunch break didn't last nearly long enough. My dad yelled out, "Breaks over everyone, time to get back to work!" There was a small grumble and groans as we stood up. My father commented, "Oh my, I shouldn't have sat down." Our moms giggled at our dads groaning and started on cleaning up the picnic area as we put on our work gloves and started back to work.

Suddenly my mother ran over to my father who was running the chainsaw. She was yelling, "Jimmy! Stop!"

My father shut off his chainsaw and asked, "What's up?"

She was still yelling, "I think we saw a person, deeper into the woods! Right down by the end of the trail!"

By this time, Lisa's dad had shut off his chainsaw to see what all the commotion was about. We all ran over and gathered around my parents, wondering what on earth was going on. As my mother explained to everyone what she had seen, Lisa and I looked at each other with worried looks. It was the first time that we thought about our creature friend. Is the creature (Alex) what our moms had seen?

My mother explained very frantically, "I just saw a man walking in the distance, further down the trail! He was really tall, and it looked like he was wearing a fur coat!"

Lisa's mom chimed in, "I saw him too! I bet he's bigger than any man any of us have ever seen!"

Our dads had concerned looks on their faces as they peered down the trail. My father said, "Let's go check it out." They both agreed and headed in that direction while our moms and us stayed close to the truck for safety.

My mother yelled out as our dads walked away, "Be careful!" We all watched nervously as they headed down the hill further up the trail until we couldn't see them any longer.

The two of our dads were out of sight for about twenty minutes. Our moms were starting to get very worried that something may have happened. My mother mentioned to us all in the truck, "I'm glad that Jimmy has his handgun with him."

Lisa and I looked at each other with surprise and fear. I whispered to Lisa, "What if they see Alex?"

To my surprise, my mother asked, "Who's Alex?"

Lisa gave me a look like I've never seen before. I wasn't sure what to say. Lisa blurted out, "He's a hermit that lives way back in the woods. He's harmless."

Both our moms replied at the same time. "A hermit?"

I chimed in, "Ya, he's a really big guy that Lisa and I sometimes leave food for."

"Food?" My mother loudly replied. "For a hermit?" She added.

Lisa's mom looked at Lisa and I with fear in her eyes and asked, "Isn't that dangerous? What if he hurt the two of you?"

Lisa answered with our creature friend, Alex, in mind, "Mom, he's the one who took care of and carried Jacob back to his father when he hit his head. He means no harm! He just enjoys living in the back of the woods and being one with nature."

My mother commented, "Why does it sound like you have talked to this, this hermit?"

"Both Jacob and I actually did talk to him for a minute, mother. He was nothing like what we expected. He's not scary at all. He just wants to enjoy the woods and to be left alone. He would never hurt anyone."

Lisa's mom said with concern, "We will have to discuss this with your fathers."

Just then Lisa said, "There they are now."

Once they returned, my mother asked, "What did you find?"

My father then filled us in, "Well, we didn't find anything, really. Something smelled like it died back by the ravine, but we couldn't find the source."

Lisa and I knew exactly what they had both smelled. Alex was here. That was a good sign for us that he wasn't hurt in the tornado.

My mother then tattled to our fathers, "Well, these two have been keeping a secret. They told us that what we saw was most likely a hermit that's been living deeper in the woods. And they have talked to this hermit as well!"

"What on earth?" My father replied.

Lisa informed them, "Alex is the one who cared for and brought Jacob back so that you would find him."

Our parents were all perplexed with what to do about this. "Well, we've wasted enough time. We'll talk more about this later but for now we have to make the most of this daylight and get some wood cut."

We all got back to work cutting and hauling wood back to the farm until the sun went down. While the rest of us unloaded the wood, our mothers whipped up some delicious fried chicken, mashed potatoes, gravy, biscuits, and sweet corn. We could smell it all the way outside by the barn.

My mother yelled out just as we were finishing up, "Dinners ready, come and get it!" Even Lisa's mom got in on the act and rang our dinner bell hanging on the porch.

My father laughed and said, "You don't have to tell me twice!"

Lisa and I raced to the back door. I was going to let her win, but she could run really fast and won on her own. I was totally fine with that. My mother reminded us all to wash up before we got to the table.

Lisa commented once we sat at the table and started passing around the dishes, "I can't believe how hungry I am. I don't think I've ever worked that hard in my life." We all gave her a little chuckle.

My father then stated, "If you are all willing, we can do this again tomorrow?"

"Sure thing!" Replied Lisa's dad.

Lisa looked at me with tired eyes. I could tell that all she wanted to do or think about was to finish dinner and then hit the bed.

It had been a very productive and exhausting day for everyone. Plus, even though Alex had been sighted, his secret was still safe.

15

THAT WAS LUCKY

Our parents scolded Lisa for not letting them know about the hermit. We were both now forbidden from talking to Alex, the hermit, ever again. We knew that Alex was not a hermit but of course our parents didn't know that. It actually made it a lot easier knowing that they thought that Alex was a hermit. Had they thought that he was a Bigfoot? I couldn't even imagine what would happen then. At least we weren't banned from going into the woods.

Having the sighting yesterday by our moms gave Lisa and I renewed hope that we would be able to find and visit Alex again.

Once we finished breakfast, everyone loaded the truck and tractor and headed for the woods again. This time Lisa and I were going to keep a sharp eye out for Alex. We were hoping we would see him but not that our parents would.

The woods seemed a little quiet as we unloaded the gear. Lisa's dad commented, "What a peaceful place!"

My father added, "Sure is! I wish I could just sit here and absorb all the nature every morning. It's good for the soul! Maybe someday we will build a small cabin up here."

Lisa and I now understand how Alex must feel when he visits our world. We live in a world where Alex and others like him want to visit the solitude and beauty of our world. I really hope to be able to talk to Alex again. Lisa and I have so many questions to ask him. But for now, our dads were signaling at us to get busy helping with the wood cutting.

Jimmy, Jacob and Lisa eating on the tree stumps

We worked hard until our moms, once again, brought us a picnic lunch. This time, they had prepared ham & cheese sandwiches and potato chips. We all sat on the cut logs around the same area as yesterday. It was actually a lot of fun, talking and listening to our parents talk. It was like we had doubled our family. Our parents were discussing Lisa's new house.

Lisa's dad stated, "The builders will be breaking ground shortly. Hopefully by the end of the week."

My mother commented with a smile, "You all are welcome to stay as long as you need!"

My father chipped in, "Yes, as long as you want." My father added, "I know that we are enjoying your company and help around the farm."

Lisa smiled at me and said, "I suppose we all should get back to work."

Lisa's mom jumped up in excitement and yelled out as she reached into the picnic basket, "Oh wait! We also made these! Ruth and I made her secret Farmhouse Cookies!" These were my favorite cookies. They were called farmhouse chocolate chip cookies. They were basically chocolate chip cookies with oatmeal, walnuts, and cornflakes mixed in. As everyone took a bite all you could hear was, "Mmmm!" Lisa looked at me with big eyes.

I asked, "Good, right?"

She shook her head "No!"

I asked, "What? You don't like them?"

She shook her head again, "No!"

I said, "Okay, then. I'll eat it if you don't like it!"

Lisa grabbed my arm and pulled me close. She whispered in my ear. "Not the cookie. I can see a portal at the end of the fallen trees."

Confused, I turned my head and looked but I didn't see anything. Our parents were getting up to start work again so Lisa and I did the same.

Once our moms headed back down to the house and our dads started up their chainsaws, I took a closer look. Sure, enough I could now see a slight shimmer at the end of the fallen trees. Our fathers were only about fifty yards from it.

Lisa asked, "What if they notice it?"

I shook my head and raised my shoulders, "I don't know."

Lisa frantically started dragging branches away. As she walked by dragging a big branch, she stated, "The portal must move around."

I said, "Ya, it's nowhere near the ravine now!"

We worked for another couple hours before our dads got so close to the portal that we had to do something. We couldn't risk them finding out that there were portals. Much less a creature that uses them as transportation to move from its dimension to ours. So, we had to think quickly!

Lisa looked at me with a weird look in her eyes. She grabbed a couple branches and started pulling them toward the brush pile when she suddenly fell and yelled out while grabbing her ankle. I ran over to her as our dads both shut down their chainsaws. Lisa yelled out in pain, "My ankle! I think I sprained it!"

Lisa's dad sat her on a log and propped up her ankle, taking off her shoe and sock to inspect her injury. As he squeezed her ankle Lisa yelled out in pain once again.

Lisa commented, "It's swollen, right?"

Her dad answered, "Doesn't look swollen. But we had better get you back to the house and get some ice on it."

My father jumped up and said, "Come on, Jacob. Let's get all the tools into the truck." As we did Lisa's dad helped her into the truck.

Once we all arrived back down to the farm, Lisa's dad helped her into the house and had her lie down on the couch. I grabbed an ice pack and put it on her ankle.

Lisa's mom was a little scared and suggested, "I think we should take her to the emergency room right away and get an X-ray."

Lisa jumped in and said, "I'm sure it's not broken, mom! I don't need to go to the emergency room. It's starting to feel better already!"

My father then wanted me to go help them empty the wood out of the truck and trailer. Our moms then went into the kitchen to finish cooking dinner. Now that we were alone, I asked Lisa, "Are you okay? You took quite the tumble."

Lisa answered, "Of course I'm okay! I'm faking it! I had to do something! I saw your father's leg disappear into the portal! He was just about to step back into it."

"Wow!" I said in shock. "Good job! It worked!" I added.

I couldn't believe how lucky we were. If it wasn't for Lisa's quick thinking, we could've had an entirely different outcome.

"What if your father had backed all the way into the portal?" Lisa asked.

I replied, "Not sure but I'm glad we don't have to find out!"

After helping our moms clean up the dinner table and dishes, Lisa and I headed to my room. Well, it was Lisa's room for now. I really didn't mind sharing my room with her, even though I had to sleep on the couch. Lisa was my best friend and whenever we weren't doing something together, I felt a little alone and bored. I always looked forward to seeing her after being apart. I felt a bond towards her that I have never felt before. I wanted to share all my thoughts with her. She was the sibling I never had but different. It was hard to explain how I felt. I just knew she was someone that I cherish and maybe I was the same to her?

16

NEW NEIGHBORS

I woke the next morning to the rumble of heavy construction equipment traveling past the farm towards Lisa's family's place. I jumped up off the couch to see semi-trucks carrying a bull-dozer and another with a large backhoe.

I quickly threw on my shoes and ran upstairs to get Lisa. She was watching out the bedroom window at all the equipment passing by. Our dads were already at work, and we could see our moms down the road where all the trucks were gathering.

I asked Lisa, "Is that where you guys are building your new house?"

Lisa replied, "Not that I'm aware of. We had better go check it out." We both ran hastily downstairs and out the door. We grabbed our bikes and rode off to see what on earth was going on.

Once we got there my mother greeted us with, "Hey kids!"

Lisa asked, "What's going on? Why are we building our new house here?"

Lisa's mom replied, "Oh sweetie, this isn't our house. This is going to be our new neighbor's home."

Lisa yelled out "What? New neighbors?"

Lisa's mom grabbed Lisa by the hand and pointed toward a man standing by the construction men in hard hats and said, "That's the dad and his wife, that is their son Jimmy walking toward us. This is going to be their new home."

Lisa asked, "But this is our property, right?"

Lisa's mom replied, "Not anymore. We had to sell some of the land to afford the upgrades to our new home. We weren't using this land anyway!" She added.

The new neighbors then walked up, and the mother introduced herself, "Hi, I'm Patty and this is my son Jimmy. Oh, and that's my husband Tim." She pointed at the tall man talking to the construction crew. He noticed and gave us a smile and a wave.

My mother then asked, "So where are your folks moving from?"

The new neighbor's mom then replied, "From Milwaukee. It's just too crowded for us. We wanted Jimmy to grow up and enjoy nature and be around folks like all you, that have small town morals."

Lisa's mom stated, "Well, I think you'll find that here! Welcome to the neighborhood!" The moms all hugged with excitement and started chatting amongst themselves.

I looked at Lisa and she did not look happy at all. Jimmy looked at me, so I reached out my hand to shake his and said, "Welcome to the neighborhood, Jimmy!" He seemed a little shy, so I asked him, "How old are you?"

"I'm going to be eleven in about a month," he replied.

"Oh, cool! You're about the same age as Lisa and I." I turned to look at Lisa, but she was already walking into the driveway of the farm. I'm not sure what got into her, but I could tell she didn't like what was happening here today.

My mother then asked me, "Hey Jacob, could you and Lisa hang out with Jimmy for a while?" I knew this wasn't a request but more like an order that I had no choice in.

I of course said, "Sure. It'll be fun!"

Jimmy and I scurried off to the farm to catch up with Lisa. We walked into the house but couldn't see her. I told Jimmy to wait in the living room while I checked upstairs in my bedroom. I reached my bedroom door to find it closed so I knocked. No answer. I knocked again. Nothing. So, I slowly opened the door to find Lisa, face down on the bed, crying. I walked over and sat on the edge of the bed. I had never dealt with someone crying like this before. I gathered up the courage to do as my mother would do if I was ever upset. I slowly started comforting Lisa by rubbing her back. I was a little afraid to touch her. I didn't know if she would get upset and shrug me away. I continued to do as my mother would do and I asked, "Are you okay? Can you tell me why you are so upset?"

Lisa continued to cry. After a minute of silence, Lisa turned her head, sniffed a few times, and said, "How come they get a home before I do?" I now knew why she was upset.

I gave a soft chuckle and explained to Lisa, "I overheard the construction crew talking as we were leaving. They were telling Jimmy's mom that they were going to work on both homes at the same time." I looked out the window and off in the distance, and said, "Look! They are down at your place now!"

Lisa popped up off the bed and wiped her eyes.

"See!" I said as I pointed out the window.

Lisa then sniffled and said, "I just want to have a place to call home. Not that your family hasn't made this feel like our home. It's just not the same."

I asked Lisa in hope that it would help her feel better, "I have to go and get my chores done. Wanna help? The animals love it when you're around!

After taking a deep breath and a sigh, Lisa replied, "Sure, I would like that! Then we can spend time together after we are done?" Lisa asked.

"Yes, that'll be cool," I replied.

We both raced down the stairs and ran into Jimmy, who I had totally forgotten about. Lisa asked with distain in her voice, "What's he doing here?"

I replied, "Our moms wanted him to hang out with us."

Lisa gave a grunt and headed right out the front door. I just shrugged my shoulders as Jimmy looked at me. He seemed a little uncomfortable with Lisa being so rude to him.

I said to Jimmy, "Don't worry about it. She'll come around." I then asked, "So, do you want to help me feed and water the animals?"

Jimmy nodded and said, "Yes, that would be awesome! I've never fed any farm animals before. Only my pet Turtle, Rufus. I am pretty sure that Rufus is much easier to take care of compared to all the animals you have here on the farm."

I smiled and commented, "It's not so bad once you get used to it!"

Jimmy and I headed out the door once again to catch up to Lisa who was already starting to water the horses. You could tell by the look on Jimmy's face that he was excited to see the horses. He cautiously reached through the fence and started petting their soft noses. I ran over to our garden and picked a few carrots for Jimmy to feed them. Jimmy was loving every minute of it. Once we fed and watered all the animals, we headed to pick up the eggs from the chicken coop.

Jimmy finally spoke, "I didn't know you could pick your own eggs?"

I laughed as Lisa rolled her eyes at him. I asked, "Where did you think eggs came from?"

"From the store," he replied.

I laughed again and explained, "Sure, but all the food products you eat all start out on a farm."

We took the basket of eggs in and handed them to our moms, including Jimmy's mom, who were all back at the house. "Are you all hungry?" my mother asked.

We all shook our heads, "Yes!" and went to wash up for breakfast.

We all gobbled down our breakfast and headed outside in search of something fun for the three of us to do together. We sat on the porch, and I asked Jimmy, "Do you have a bike here?"

Jimmy replied, "I do. It's in the back of our truck. I can go grab it out."

"Great!" I replied.

Lisa and I grabbed our bikes and we went off down the road, passing both busy construction sites. Lisa, you can tell was starting to lighten up a little bit. However, Lisa still hadn't said a word to Jimmy though.

We reached the next county road after riding about two miles. "Which way, Jacob?" asked Lisa.

"I know! Let's go right!" I replied. We all took off and headed toward the lake. It was only a couple miles up the road. There were always a lot of summer vacationers there from Illinois. They would have small cottages or a mobile home to stay in on their getaways from the big cities like Chicago and Milwaukee. Plus, there is an awesome tourist destination nearby. Wisconsin Dells has so many attractions like water parks, go carts, a haunted house, boat tours of the river, and so many novelty restaurants and shops. The list literally goes on and on.

Once at the lake, the three of us pulled up by the beach and saw a few kids swimming, though there was nobody we knew.

Lisa yelled out as she dropped her bike, "Who wants to go swimming?"

Jimmy and I looked at each other, quickly jumped off our bikes and ran into the water. Lisa had already started swimming out to the diving raft that was out deeper in the swimming area. Jimmy and I raced each other to the raft. He was a little taller than I was, but I was able to barely beat him.

Lisa chimed in with a slight insult as we climbed onto the raft, "You almost got beat by the new kid."

I quickly responded with, "You think so, huh!" as I grabbed her and threw her into the water. We all laughed and swam together in the water for about twenty minutes.

The three of us were relaxing on the raft when I saw a few kids about our age jump into the water and swim our way. They climbed up onto the raft and started talking about us. We couldn't hear what they were saying.

Of course, Lisa jumped up and ranted toward the other kids, "Excuse me! What are you saying about us?"

The other kids stood up and one of the girls replied defensively, "Sorry, I just thought that your friend (pointing at me) was cute! That's all!"

Lisa rifled back aggressively toward the girl, "Well, keep your opinions to yourself!" Lisa looked at Jimmy and I, and said loudly, "Let's go, you two!" Lisa hastily jumped in the water as Jimmy and I both said "Sorry!" to the girl and her friends before jumping into the water. It was obvious that Lisa was still in a mood. Jimmy and I did not understand why she was so mean to the girl and her friends.

Once back at the shore we all met at the bikes where I asked Lisa, "What has gotten into you today?"

Lisa shook her head, climbed onto her bike, and took off.

Jimmy asked, "Is she always like this?"

"Not really," I replied as we took off to catch up to Lisa.

We rode our bikes about halfway home when Jimmy shouted out, "Hey guys! What was that noise in the woods?"

Neither Lisa nor I heard anything. We kept riding when we all heard a large tree branch break. "Whoa! I heard that!" I shouted.

We all stopped and listened for a few seconds. There was nothing. Lisa and I looked at each other. "Maybe it's Alex." Lisa commented,

"Maybe?" I replied.

Jimmy asked, "Who's Alex?"

"Just a hermit who lives in the woods," Lisa answered as we started riding again.

We were almost home when Jimmy yelled out, "I think I just saw the hermit, guys! He just walked across the edge of the woods by that row of pine trees!" We all kept looking but saw nothing. Jimmy continued, "He was really tall and fast! He was wearing a coat! It looked like a fur coat. He has to be hot wearing a coat like that."

Lisa commented, "Well, that must be Alex!"

We continued our ride home with no more sightings of Alex.

Once home we parked our bikes and ran into the house where all of our parents were getting ready to eat dinner. Much to our surprise, my mother announced, "We are having the Morgans stay overnight tonight. So, Lisa and Jimmy, you will be camping out in the living room with Jacob tonight."

Jimmy spoke up and said jokingly, "Do we get to have a campfire in here too?" Everyone laughed, including Jimmy. What came out of his mouth next shocked everyone. "Can we invite the hermit?"

Jimmy's mother asked with concern in her voice, "Hermit? What hermit?"

My mother put her at ease and explained, "It's just some guy that likes to live off the grid deep in the woods. He actually helped Jacob when he fell and hit his head. This hermit carried Jacob back to an area where his father could find him."

"Oh my!" Replied Jimmy's mother.

"If it wasn't for this hermit guy, Jacob could have been in real trouble." My mother added.

Jimmy's dad commented, "Maybe we all could hire this, this, hermit guy to help with things around the farms."

Lisa jumped into the conversation and said, "His name is Alex. He also doesn't want a job. He likes living off the land and doesn't want to be bothered by anyone."

"Okay then! We will leave him alone," replied Jimmy's dad.

We all finished our dinner and set up our spots in the living room for the night. Jimmy and I put sleeping bags on the floor, and I gave Lisa the soft couch. I even tried to help her set it up, but she snapped at me, "Just because I'm a girl, doesn't mean I can't do things myself!"

I replied cautiously, "Sorry, I was just trying to be a gentleman."

Jimmy snickered as he got into his sleeping bag. Lisa and I followed suit.

All our parents headed to bed as well. I really enjoy having such a full house. It seemed as though our family had now just tripled, although I knew this wasn't going to last forever, but it was nice having it for now. It really broke the routine of having just my parents and me. The farm was much livelier. It was also fun listening to all of our parents talk, laugh, and tell stories.

As I started to fall asleep, I felt a hand grab mine, and Lisa said softly, "I'm sorry, Jacob."

I whispered back, "It's okay."

From the darkness, Jimmy blurted out loudly, "What about me? Are you sorry for being mean to me?"

Lisa snapped back in a funny way, "Shut up Jimmy!" The three of us laughed and fell asleep with smiles on our faces.

17

PINKY SWEAR

The next morning, we woke to a lot of commotion coming from the kitchen. I guess this is what is to be expected with three families now living in the same house. I was also very happy that we had two bathrooms. Lisa's dad and my father were taking off to work and all our moms and Jimmy's dad were setting up the table for our breakfast. The smell was incredible, not like bacon or even pancakes, but more like the smell of a bakery. The three of us jumped up, put our sleeping bags away and washed up for breakfast. As we sat at the table, I couldn't believe my eyes. There were large cinnamon rolls all smothered in icing on each of our plates.

I excitedly expressed, "Now this is my kind of breakfast!"

My mother announced, "Don't get too used to this Jacob!"

I had the biggest smile and couldn't wait to get started on it. It tasted even better than it looked. Jimmy's mom was quite the baker. We gobbled down the cinnamon rolls and just as every day of my life, we headed out to the barn where the three of us worked on my daily chores of taking care of the animals. Having help from Lisa and Jimmy really makes my life easy. It also made more time for all of us to hang out together.

Jacob, Lisa and Jimmy, pinky swear

We could hear the construction crews working hard building Jimmy's new home. We grabbed our bikes and headed to Jimmy's new home. Things were moving along quite well. They had the basement walls built and were working on the ground floor. I looked over at Lisa and she was looking a little sad.

I asked, "What's up? You look a little down."

Lisa replied, "I just wish they were working on my house."

Just then one of the crew walked by us carrying some boards and said, "We have a crew working over there as well."

Lisa's face perked up as she immediately jumped back on her bike. Jimmy and I jumped onto our bikes and the three of us made our way to Lisa's place.

Sure enough, they were even further along than Jimmy's home. Lisa had the biggest smile as she gazed upon her new home being built. She pointed at the second story and yelled out very excitedly, "That's going to be my bedroom!" At that moment I realized that Lisa's mood lately was because she really had no place to call home. We walked around the house checking it out. Lisa was just in awe at how nice her new home was going to be. I was happy that she could now have something to look forward to.

Once we were done admiring the house Jimmy asked, "What do you guys want to do now?"

Lisa with a smile asked to my surprise, "Why don't we go find Alex?"

I replied, "I'm not sure if that's a good idea. We have Jimmy with us."

Jimmy responded, "I'm game to go find the hermit. It's not like he's dangerous, right?"

Lisa and I looked at each other and shrugged our shoulders in a sort of agreement. "Okay, let's go." I said as we all started off back to the farm.

Once back at the farm I yelled into the door, "Hey mom, the three of us are going for a hike in the woods."

My mother yelled back, "You kids stay away from the hermit! And be back by dinner time!"

"Okay, we will." I replied as I jumped off the porch, skipping all the stairs.

Lisa then reminded me, "Hey, we should have a treat for Alex!"

"You're right!" I replied. I quickly ran into the house and grabbed some granola bars and a few bottles of water for us and threw them into my backpack.

The three of us rode through the farm, past the corn field that was now about five feet tall, and up the hill toward the woods. Once at the top of the hill Lisa and I blocked the trail with our bikes.

Jimmy pulled up and asked, "What's up? Why are we stopped?"

Lisa looked and nodded to me. I knew what she meant. We needed to make sure Jimmy was on the same page as the two of us. I knew I had to be upfront and honest with him.

I took a deep breath and started out with, "Jimmy, what I'm about to tell you might sound a little crazy. You also can't tell a soul about anything that you may see or happens up here." I added. "You have to swear on your life!"

Jimmy replied with low expectations of what he thought I may be talking about, "Okay, no problem. I won't say anything."

Lisa wasn't satisfied and said, "No Jimmy, you have to swear on your life that you won't ever say a word about this!"

Jimmy was a little confused after just swearing he wouldn't say anything but confirmed as he reached out to the two of us, "I pinky swear. I won't say a word to anyone, ever!" As Jimmy reached out, we all wrapped our pinkie fingers together and shook our hands to bond the secret to never be told outside our circle of three.

I took another deep breath and pointed toward the woods, "This is a very special place, Jimmy. This is where Alex likes to visit because where he lives there are no tall trees. Alex likes to hang out here without humans bugging him."

Jimmy quickly asked, "What do you mean without humans? You say that like he's not human!"

Lisa replied to Jimmy, "Well, he's not! He's a Bigfoot!"

"What?" Yells Jimmy as he looks at the two of us. He could tell that we were not kidding. "A real Bigfoot? Like that show I saw on TV?" Jimmy asked.

Both Lisa and I nodded our heads and confirmed to Jimmy that we were saying, yes, a real, live Bigfoot.

Jimmy's mouth was wide open in surprise as his eyes scanned around the woods in, somewhat, disbelief.

Lisa reminds Jimmy, "Remember what you swore. You can't tell a soul."

Jimmy nods and says, "Oh trust me, I won't. I promise! Everyone will think that I'm crazy! So, where is this, Alex?" Jimmy asked.

Lisa responded, "We're not sure exactly. He could be anywhere!"

I added, "We'll have to look around for him. We're not sure if he'll show himself to us, especially since you're with us."

Jimmy, unfettered, said, "Well! What are we waiting for? Let's find him! I've never seen a Bigfoot before!"

Lisa and I chuckled a little at how excited Jimmy was about this. Lisa and I knew that if we did find Alex, that Jimmy might not be able to handle the sight of a real, live Bigfoot. We also hoped that Alex would be receptive of us telling and actually bringing Jimmy into the fold.

We all started walking around the area where we last saw the portal. Lisa and I walked in a circle around the area but saw nothing out of the ordinary.

Jimmy noticed and asked, "What on earth are you guys looking for? I thought we were looking for a Bigfoot?"

Lisa looked at me and told him the truth, "Jimmy, we're looking for a portal."

Jimmy took a step back and said in shock, "A portal? Now there's a portal as well? This day just keeps getting better! Are you guys sure you're not pulling my leg?"

Lisa and I shook our heads, "No!" I added, "Alex comes from a different dimension to spend time in ours."

Jimmy just shook his head in disbelief, smiled and started walking back toward our bikes.

I asked, "Where are you going?"

"Home! You guys had me going for a minute but now I know that both of you are just trying to mess with me!" Jimmy replied.

Lisa and I both ran after him. Lisa grabbed his arm and spun Jimmy back around and said, "Nope, you're coming with us! There're no take backs on our promise!"

Jimmy responded, "Ya, that's when Alex was a human that lives in the woods! Not a Bigfoot that travels from another dimension through portals!"

I jumped in and said, "It doesn't matter, Jimmy! You pinky swore and we're holding you to it!"

Jimmy thought about it for a second and asked, "Are there any other secrets I don't know about or is any of it true?"

Lisa replied, "Nothing! No more secrets! Alex and the portal are absolutely true! We promise!"

Jimmy held out his hand and said, "Now, we need to pinky swear again to keep all our secrets!"

Lisa and I glanced at each other, smiled and pinky swore once again with Jimmy.

We started searching the area and explaining all our previous happenings with Alex to Jimmy. We couldn't find Alex or any signs of a portal.

Lisa yelled over toward Jimmy and I, "What do you think about heading over to the ravine?"

"I don't think we have enough time for that." I replied.

We made our way back to the head of the trail and jumped on our bikes. Lisa took off and yelled, "Last one back has to do ten pushups!"

Jimmy and I looked at each other and took off! I knew the hill well, so I easily caught up to Lisa and passed her. Jimmy was catching her as well. I slid my bike sideways as I reached the house. It was going to be close. Both were even coming past the barn. You could see the determination on both of their faces. Neither one of them wanted to lose. Jimmy gave a final push and passed Lisa at the very end.

"Good hustle guys!" I commented.

Jimmy said between deep breaths, "Looks like Lisa owes us ten push-ups!"

Lisa looked up with distaste in her eyes. She set her bike down and proceeded to do the pushups.

Jimmy and I started the countdown midway, "Five, four, three, two, and one."

Jimmy and I cheered as Lisa rolled over onto her back and said, "I really hate you guys!" Jimmy and I laughed, followed by Lisa chuckling.

Jimmy spoke up and asked, "Can we do this again tomorrow?"

As Lisa and I smiled in confirmation to Jimmy's question, we could hear my mother yell, "Kids! It's time for dinner!"

I yelled back, "Okay, be right there!" I then reminded Jimmy, "You can't say a word about any of this to anyone, Jimmy."

Jimmy replied, "Not sure what you're talking about but let's eat!" The three of us laughed at Jimmy's sarcasm and raced up the porch steps and into the house toward the smell of fried chicken.

18

PORTAL DANGER

Today is going to be the day we find Alex again and show Jimmy a real, live, Bigfoot. After the three of us were done with chores and breakfast, we once again grabbed our bikes and headed for the woods. It was so peaceful riding the trail toward the ravine; the birds chirping, squirrels scurrying, and the sunlight glittering through the trees onto the forest floor. The air was cool, with a slight breeze blowing in our faces, when suddenly there was a terrible smell. Almost simultaneously, all three of us had the most disgusting look upon our faces that stopped us in our tracks. I even pulled my shirt up to cover my nose.

Jimmy asked while doing the same, "What on earth is that horrible smell? It's worse than our garbage can after a sweltering summer day!"

Lisa replied, "I think Alex is close!"

"Oh ya! That's right, doesn't a Bigfoot smell really bad?" asked Jimmy.

Lisa rolled her eyes and replied, "A Bigfoot doesn't smell bad. I didn't notice any overpowering smell when we talked to Alex before. However, I did notice that there was an awful smell when we were near the portal."

I added, "You know what. I noticed the same thing. Also, I overheard my mother say to my father that his clothes really stunk the day he almost stepped into the portal."

Lisa commented, "It must be the portal that stinks. It has to be close! Let's spread out and quietly look around."

It then popped in my mind that the night the Bigfoot cared for me, I must have been taken into their world. That's why my parents couldn't find me. I did feel like a static charge when Alex brought me back to my father. We must have been going through the portal, meaning I stayed in their world overnight. I wasn't sure how to feel about it.

The three of us spread out and searched high and low trying to find the portal. After about fifteen minutes of unsuccessful searching, Lisa and I met back where we had left our bikes. We waited a few minutes for Jimmy but he was a no show.

After about ten more minutes I told Lisa, "I'm getting a little worried. We're going to have to go look around and find him before he really gets lost."

Lisa agreed and we went off in the direction we last saw him. We walked back and forth in a grid pattern but to no avail. "Where on earth could that boy have gone?" Lisa asked. We then moved on to another area where I had noticed some footprints heading off further into the woods. "He must have gone this way!" Lisa commented. "I think the smell is getting worse, Jacob! We must be getting close to the portal." Lisa added. Sure enough. There was the portal behind a couple of small pines. But where was Jimmy?

We searched the area all around the portal, making sure not to get too close. The last thing we wanted was to step into it and have to deal with the wild creatures that Alex had warned us about that lived in his world. We kept an eye out for Alex as well. Maybe he knows where Jimmy was.

Lisa sat on a stump and asked, "You don't think that Jimmy was dumb enough to go into the portal, do you?"

She had me thinking now. "I don't think so. Maybe he accidentally stepped into it and can't find his way back?" I replied.

We waited for about thirty more minutes before Lisa started yelling, "I can't wait any longer! Jimmy, where are you?"

We listened but got no reply. So, I yelled out as well, "Jimmy! Jimmy! Can you hear me?" Still no reply.

"I'm really worried Jacob!" stated Lisa.

"Me too!" I replied.

Lisa asked, "What are we going to do?"

I thought for a second and replied, "I've got an idea but you're not going to like it."

Lisa looked at me with great concern and said, "No way! We aren't going through the portal! It's too dangerous Jacob!"

I replied, "I have some rope in my backpack. I'll wrap one end around me and one to this tree next to the portal. I'll walk through and see if I can find Jimmy."

Lisa was shaking her head and replied, "No, we should go get help!"

"We don't have time!" I replied back as I tied the rope around myself and then the tree. Slowly, I approached the portal. I looked back and said to Lisa, "If I have any trouble, I'll tug on the rope three times. Then pull me back. If you can't, then go get help!"

Lisa nodded because, she couldn't even speak out of fear at this point.

I slowly stepped into the portal. My skin started to tingle. It was like static electricity. I remember that feeling from when Alex carried me to my father. For a few seconds I couldn't see anything. I kept stepping forward through the portal. I was beginning to think I had made a big mistake. I suddenly could see something from the other side. It was very blurry. I couldn't make out what it was. I continued to move forward. The object started to come into focus as I continued to move toward it. It was a giant rock with some small bushes around it.

I took another step forward and I was now completely out of the portal. I very nervously looked around, searching for Jimmy. I walked up to the rock and peered around it. Alex was right about there not being any large trees in his world. There was nothing but brush growing. I looked up and noticed the sky was much dimmer than in our world. I also noticed that the air smelled different as well. Not as clean and crisp as what I was used to. I didn't hear anything either. No animal or bird sounds.

I finally got the courage to see if Jimmy could hear me. I softly said, "Jimmy! Jimmy! Can you hear me?" I heard nothing. So, I tried a little louder, "Jimmy! Can you hear me?" Still nothing! I decided to move to another cropping of bushes. I looked around for Jimmy before calling out for him. I still saw nothing. I called out again. Still nothing. I moved out to what was a large cliff. Something started to look familiar to me as I looked down. It was the ravine! The same landscape as in our world, minus all the tall trees. I found that Alex's world was exactly like ours. Just smaller vegetation.

I then noticed something moving down by the creek at the bottom. It was Jimmy! I couldn't believe it! I found him! I was afraid to yell too loud and alert a dangerous creature, so I grabbed a rock and threw it down toward Jimmy. It landed about twenty feet from him. Jimmy spun around and looked scared. I waved but he didn't see me. I grabbed another rock and threw it between us. He ducked down and looked in my direction. I waved again. This time he saw me. I waved for him to come to me.

Jimmy pointed in the other direction. I looked around and saw more movement off to the right. I noticed Jimmy started making his way toward me but what looked like a large bear was moving toward him. I had to help Jimmy get up here before this creature caught up with him. I had to think quickly! I grabbed a rock and threw it as far as I could. It landed in the creek just past the creature. The creature spun around and dove into the creek, looking for what I had thrown. I waved to Jimmy to hurry up! He was hustling as fast as he could. The creature noticed Jimmy. It let out a loud growl and started lunging toward Jimmy. I yelled, "Jimmy! Hurry! It sees you!"

Jimmy ran up to me all out of breath. I grabbed him and we ran into the portal without saying a word. We came flying out the other side and landed on the ground at Lisa's feet.

Lisa yelled, "Oh my goodness, you guys. You've had me worried out of my mind. What happened over there?"

Jimmy and I got up and untied the rope from the stump and myself before hearing a deep, loud growl from the portal. Lisa's eyes bugged out and she asked with fear, "What was that?"

I quickly replied, "It's a creature that Jimmy barely got away from!"

"We have to get out of here!" Jimmy added.

We ran to our bikes and started riding as fast as we could back toward the farm. We reached the trailhead at the edge of woods. We could see the farm below. I took a quick look back to make sure that the creature hadn't followed us. I saw nothing.

I reminded everyone, "You guys, we can't say a word about this to anyone!"

Jimmy and Lisa nodded in agreement. I could tell by Jimmy's face that he was still in shock.

Lisa rambled off a few questions since she was out of the loop, "What happened back there? Why did you go through the portal Jimmy? What kind of creature was chasing you guys?"

I jumped in and said, "Let's get back to the farm and we can go over everything that happened." We took off and raced down the hill back to the farm.

We pulled up to the front porch to find all our moms hanging out enjoying an iced tea. Jimmy's mom asked, "How was your hike today? You are all staying away from the hermit?" We looked at each other and nodded in agreement.

My mother reminded us, "You kids make sure to do the chores and get washed up for dinner." My mother added. "You three smell like you ran into a skunk!"

We worked together and knocked out the chores quickly so we could talk about what had happened. The three of us sat down by our fire pit behind the woodshed where Lisa anxiously asked, "I need to know what happened to you two in Alex's world!"

"Ya, Jimmy! How did you end up over there?" I asked.

Jimmy took a deep breath and started explaining, "Well, I was searching for the portal, but I didn't realize I had found it until I accidentally walked right into it." Jimmy added. "Once I was in it, I got turned around and ended up on the other side."

Lisa asked, "Why didn't you come right back? We warned you it would be dangerous to go through it!"

Jimmy responded, "I guess my curiosity got the best of me. I just wanted to look around a little."

I asked, "How did you get all the way down to the bottom of the ravine?"

"I slipped and tumbled down." Jimmy answered.

"Wait a second!" Lisa blurted out. "There is a ravine? Like our ravine? In Alex's world?" She asked.

"There is. Just no big trees, like in our world though," I replied.

Lisa jumped up and asked, "What about the creature that was chasing Jimmy?"

"It was like a bear but not quite a bear that we have here," Jimmy replied. "It had long fangs. You know, like on a saber-tooth tiger," Jimmy added.

"Oh, my goodness!" Lisa commented.

The sabre-tooth bear

We could then hear my mother ringing the dinner bell. We all started heading for the house toward the smell of chicken and dumplings! I reminded everyone, "Guys, we can't say a word about this to anyone!"

Jimmy replied, "Like they would believe us anyway!"

Lisa added with sarcasm, "Ya, they would lock us up in the loony bin and throw away the key."

We washed up thoroughly, changed our clothes and sat down for dinner. The first thing out of my father's mouth, "So kids, how was your hike in the woods today? Isn't nature peaceful up there?"

The three of us took a big gulp and Lisa answered with a smile on her face, "Oh yes! It's totally a different world up there!" Jimmy and I looked at each other and then at Lisa with eyes of disbelief that she had just said that. Lisa added, "These two boys think they can scare me with tales of giant bears with teeth like a saber-tooth tiger. They don't scare me." Everyone chuckled a little except Jimmy and I.

My mother responded, "You boys be nice to Lisa."

I replied, "We will." I just wanted to get this conversation over before Lisa gave out any more information.

Once dinner was over our parents started playing cards while the three of us went out to the front porch. Immediately I asked Lisa, "What on earth did you think you were doing?"

Jimmy added, "Ya, what the heck? Are you trying to get us in trouble?"

Lisa replied, "I knew they wouldn't believe me even if I told them some of the truth. And I was right!"

"You were lucky," I replied.

All of a sudden Lisa yelled out, "Did you guys see that?" Jimmy and I jumped up, ready to hide in the house. Lisa laughed, "You boys are awfully jumpy. It was just a shooting star!" Jimmy and I gave a huge sigh of relief. Lisa said with excitement in her eyes, "Let's lay on the porch roof and watch for more shooting stars."

I replied, "Just as long as you quit giving secrets to our parents."

"Sure. Not a problem. Now let's get up there," Lisa replied.

The three of us watched for a couple hours, in awe of the night sky before going to bed. We saw several shooting stars. We also evaluated each other on the names and where the constellations were in the night sky. What a curious and wonderful world we live in. We as a race of humans are so busy with just getting by, that we tend to miss so much of our world's beauty.

19

KILLER ON THE LOOSE

The next morning, we woke to a lot of commotion in the house. I shook off my sleepiness and walked into the kitchen where all our parents were chattering loudly about something. I rubbed my eyes as I was stretching and asked, "Morning! What's going on?"

"Well, according to the radio, a big bear was spotted over on the Fischer farm! It had killed one of their prized dairy cows," my father stated.

My mother added, "You kids stay near the farm. No running off to the woods until this killer bear is taken care of."

I think my eyes were about to pop out from my head at this news. I quickly ran into the living room to wake up Jimmy and Lisa.

Jimmy asked as I shook him awake, "What's going on?"

I replied, "I'll fill you in outside!" They both could tell this was serious as they hurried to get dressed and met me over by the fire pit. I then explained what news I had been told.

Lisa commented, "I sure hope it's not, but this must be the bear that was chasing Jimmy! It must have made it through the portal into our world!"

Jimmy asked, "What are we going to do?"

I replied, "Before anything else happens, we have to find Alex and hope he can help us!"

Lisa quickly asked, "How are we going to do that when we're not allowed to leave the farm?"

Jimmy chimed in with some fear to his tone, "Ya, I'm not going back up there ever again! You can't ever make me go back into those woods!" Lisa and I both understood Jimmy's fear, but we had to do something!

My mother stepped out onto the porch and yelled out, "Jacob, your father wants you guys to put all the animals in the stalls in the barn and lock it up until it's safe."

"Okay. That's a good idea," I replied.

The three of us gathered up all the animals and put them into the barn. It was a little crowded, but we managed. "I've got an idea!" I said as I closed up and secured the barn doors with a two by six board. You can never be too careful when it comes to a predator on the loose, especially one that we have never encountered before. "After breakfast I'll go up there with my bike and try to find Alex!" I added.

Lisa shouted, "You can't go up there by yourself!"

"Ya, are you crazy!" Jimmy added. Just then my mother yelled for us to come inside and eat breakfast.

We sat down for breakfast, still pondering how we were going to get up there safely without anyone finding out. Our luck was about to change.

Lisa's mother announced, "Hey kids, us ladies are going dress shopping this morning in town, unless you would rather us stay until the coast is clear?"

Lisa popped up and said, "No, go have fun. We'll stay here in the house until you get back from shopping."

My mother replied "Well, okay. You kids must promise to stay here in the house."

Lisa's mom asked, "Unless you kids want to come with us to town?"

We all shook our heads, "No!"

"The three of us can hang out and watch a movie or something," I stated.

Once breakfast was all cleaned up, the moms all jumped into the car and took off to town. We quickly gathered a few supplies and our backpacks and headed out the door. Lisa and I jumped onto our bikes and noticed Jimmy was still standing on the porch. He was staring off toward the woods with a blank look in his eyes.

I asked, "Jimmy, what are you doing? We gotta get going!"

Jimmy still stood there, shaking his head in a state of fear, "No!"

Lisa blurted out, "What?"

Jimmy finally spoke, "I'm not going up there! You guys shouldn't either!"

"We have to find Alex to help with the bear from his world," I replied.

Lisa added, "Alex will know what to do!"

"I'm staying here!" replied Jimmy.

Lisa said, "Let's go Jacob! We don't have much time." The two of us started off toward the woods. We were both very nervous for good reason. If we ran into this bear, I wasn't sure what we would do.

Once we reached the hilltop at the trailhead, Lisa and I stopped to surveil the area for any danger. We would need to be very cautious and hope we could find Alex before the bear finds us. We were taking a very dangerous risk.

We slowly and quietly made our way toward the ravine. Everything seemed normal as we approached the area. The birds were chirping above and squirrels were scurrying up the trees. Sure enough, the portal was still in the same spot as before. That is going to save us time not having to search for it again. That's how we ended up in this predicament.

Lisa and I stayed together as we walked around the area looking for Alex. There was no sign of him anywhere. I whispered to Lisa, "I have an idea. Let's check to see if he's..."

Just then Lisa interrupted me, "Yes, that a good idea!" Yet her mouth didn't move! I heard her in my head. She knew what I was thinking before I could even finish my sentence. While I had a confused look on my face, Lisa had a big smile on hers. Just then I got it! Already, Lisa was nodding with confirmation. This meant that Alex was nearby. We looked around but didn't see him.

Lisa told me via telepathy, "Lets both focus and ask him to come to us."

I agreed and we both took a deep breath and focused on Alex meeting us here. We waited a few minutes to no avail.

We suddenly heard something rustling in the brush off in the distance. Lisa and I looked at each other and took a big gulp of air. This had better not be the bear. "It has to be Alex. He must have heard us." Lisa said telepathically. Lisa looked at me with anticipation that we would find him, and he could help us rid our world of the dangerous bear that surely did not belong here.

Suddenly, Lisa grabbed my arm very tightly and tugged me down toward the ground. It wasn't Alex that was making its way toward us. It was the saber-tooth bear!

We didn't know what to do! Lisa and I looked at each other with fear in our eyes. I grabbed Lisa's hand and pulled her behind a big pine tree. We were lucky so far. The bear hadn't seen us. The bear was foraging for food as it made its way closer and closer to us. The bear suddenly stopped, raised its head, and started sniffing the air. I think it could smell us. It started grunting as it stood on its hind legs and continued to sniff the air. Lisa was squeezing my arm so tight that it was going numb. I could read Lisa's mind. She was in total fear.

The bear then looked in our direction and gave a thunderous growl that could be heard for a mile. It had seen us and started charging our way! Lisa and I started running away as fast as we could. There was no way we could outrun this bear. We could hear it closing fast as it crashed through the brush and small trees.

I told Lisa, "Head for your bike and race home! I'll distract it!"

Lisa looked at me knowing we had no time to waste and did as I suggested. I could hear Lisa's thoughts. She was thinking how much she didn't want to leave me alone. Also, she prayed that I would survive this bear.

The bear started to chase her so I yelled as loud as I could, "Over here! Come get me!" It worked! The bear came rushing toward me. I ran faster than I've ever run before. I could see out from the corner of my eye, Lisa racing off on her bike toward the farm. I had to figure out something, and fast! Just then I saw a large blur fly by me. Then there was a loud grunt and trees breaking. I stopped and looked back. It was Alex! He was fighting with the bear. There was so much noise. I wasn't sure who was winning. The bear then suddenly was on top with its mouth wide open. Alex was holding the bear back just enough to prevent it from biting him with those long saber-tooth, teeth. I had to help. I grabbed a large rock and ran close enough to be able to hit the bear. I threw it as hard as I could. The bear whined in pain as it backed off Alex. It turned toward me and started to charge toward me. From behind, Alex jumped onto the bear and gripped it tightly around the neck. The bear collapsed, gasping for air. I then felt the presence of something behind me. I was scared that maybe there was more than one bear. I slowly turned around. I couldn't believe what I was seeing. It was two more creatures! They were just like Alex. They rushed past me to assist Alex with the bear.

The two other Bigfoot grabbed the drowsy bear and started to drag it off toward the portal. Alex lifted his head and looked at me. He was telling me, "You are safe now."

I said, "Thank you for saving us, Alex!"

He quickly replied, "You named me Alex?"

I responded telepathically, "Yes, it was Lisa's idea. I hope that it's okay with you?"

Alex replied, "I understand that it is a special name for Lisa so you may call me Alex. Now, tell me how the creature ended up in your world."

I took a deep breath and explained the whole situation to him. Alex was very disappointed that we allowed Jimmy to know about him, the portals and his world. I assured him that Jimmy would never indulge any information to anyone else.

Just then, we could hear our truck come racing up the trail toward us. Alex took off and hid from sight behind a large thicket of trees. I thought that Lisa had told our moms that there was trouble, and they were driving the truck. As the truck pulled up, I couldn't believe my eyes! It was Lisa and Jimmy was the one driving!

They jumped out and Lisa ran to me and gave me a big hug. "I'm so glad that you're alright!" Lisa yelled.

"I'm good! Thanks to Alex and two of his friends!" I replied.

Lisa looked around and said, "Alex, you have two friends?"

Then from out behind the thicket of large trees stepped Alex. Jimmy's jaw dropped as Alex walked over to the three of us. "Yes, the other two are of my blood. They are family. I have several more that choose not to come to your world."

I said, "Well, thank you for helping us and sharing so much about yourself with us."

Lisa added, "By the way, this is our friend and new neighbor, Jimmy!"

Alex looked at Jimmy and nodded his head as a greeting. Jimmy just stood there, like a deer in headlights. I walked over to him, put my hands on both of his shoulders as his gaze never faltered at Alex and said, "Jimmy, Alex would never hurt us!"

"Ya, snap out of it, Jimmy!" Lisa added. Jimmy blinked his eyes a couple times and took a deep breath.

I gave a little chuckle and said to Jimmy, "I didn't know you could drive the truck and thanks for coming to my rescue." Jimmy then shook his head with a confused look on his face as he put his hand over his mouth. He just realized we're talking telepathically without actually speaking.

Jimmy then smiled and said, "Whoa! This is crazy, you guys!" We then heard a whistle come from Alex. He was calling the other two Bigfoot that had drug off the bear. They both stepped out from behind a heavily wooded spot near the portal and approached us. I noticed when they both walked over to Alex and touched his arm in a sort of silent greeting. Alex nodded to both as they did but didn't pick up anything being said telepathically.

Alex motioned and told us to sit on the ground. The three of them joined us in a circle. This still was quite the sensory overload for the three of us. Jimmy once again was quiet, with his jaw wide open. Alex introduced his family, "This is my sister, Haman, and her mate, Krocko. The three of us enjoy your world and are spiritual leaders to humans. Our species have been encouraged to be watchers and educators over the forests and selected humans of your world."

"Oh wow! That's awesome!" stated Lisa.

I asked, "How long have you been teaching our people?"

"We have been sending watchers since the beginning of time. We give messages and advice to the select few that we can trust in hopes that more will follow," Alex replied.

Lisa then stated, "I don't think that humans are following your advice! Not with all the pollution, crime, and destruction that we have around the world!"

Alex explained, "That is why we have chosen you to help us. Our kind will be more involved now due to everything Lisa just mentioned. Your world is now affecting our world in a negative way."

Alex's sister touched his arm and spoke up, "Our worlds are very special. There is nowhere like this. We must now do all we can to protect both worlds so that we both don't lose them. If one goes, they both do!"

Jimmy asked, "How do we do that though? We are just kids!"

"It will be a lifelong endeavor, but we can talk more about that tomorrow," Alex replied.

Lisa commented, "That's a good idea since we're not supposed to leave the house!"

As Alex and his family got up and headed toward the portal, he said, "Remember, don't go into the portal. Humans are not meant for our world and terrible things can happen."

Jimmy responded as the three of us shook our heads in agreement, "One hundred percent! I will never go there again!"

The three of us piled into the truck and I drove us back to the farm. On our way I asked, "Where did you learn how to drive, Jimmy?"

"My grandpa taught me. He had a truck like this and whenever we visited, he would show me how to drive it," Jimmy explained. "I sure do miss him!" Jimmy added. Lisa's rubbed Jimmy's back to console him.

We parked the truck and ran into the house just in time. Our moms were just arriving back from dress shopping.

20

AMBASSADORS

It sure was a crazy day yesterday. The three of us stayed up late last night just talking about how special it was for us to be chosen by Alex. We are just kids, after all! The task seemed very daunting for three eleven-year-olds. We weren't sure how Alex wanted us to get out his message to others, but we sure are excited to get started.

We were eating breakfast when Jimmy's mom asked, "Did you kids hear the good news?" We all looked at each other and shrugged our shoulders. "The Game and Wildlife Department caught that killer bear they've been looking for!"

My mom chimed in, "Ya, it was a rouge black bear! It must have wandered out of Canada since one has never been sighted here in decades."

Lisa's mom stated, "I think I heard they were going to take it back up there where it belongs."

The three of us looked at each other a little confused. It then came to me that Alex had something to do with this. Alex must have put a black bear to take the fall for the saber-tooth bear from his world. This is great news for us. Now our parents would allow us to go back into the woods without fear of a bear attack.

After breakfast, the three of us got all our chores done, grabbed our backpacks and bikes and met over by the fire pit. We were nervous but very excited to be a part of something that the three of us felt to be so worthy. Our minds were running crazy about the three of us helping to save our worlds. We just didn't want to disappoint Alex and the rest of his kind.

We rode up the hill and stopped at the top, turned our bikes around and for a minute we took in the view we have over the farm below. We could see across the valley for miles. Lisa stated, "I can't believe that the three of us are in charge of all of this!"

"Ya, I hope we can help Alex make our world a better place," Jimmy added. We turned our bikes back toward the woods and headed up the trail for the ravine to meet with Alex.

Once we reached the portal, we found a rock sitting on a stump. Under the rock was a branch pointing north. "I think that Alex wants us to go in that direction," I spoke. The forest was thick with trees, so we dropped our bikes and started hiking in the direction the stick was pointing. I had never been in this part of our woods before.

We walked for about thirty minutes with no sign of Alex. I was hoping we were headed in the right direction. I had never been this far back in our woods before. We continued walking until we reached a cliff face that soared over the forest. Lisa asked me, "Are you sure we should have gone in this direction, Jacob?"

"I'm not sure," I replied.

We looked around for any sign of Alex. Lisa said as she laid on the ground, "I'm tired!"

Jimmy stated as he sat down by Lisa, "Me too!" It seemed that we were already discouraged about helping Alex.

While the two of them rested, I continued to search around the rock face that continued both ways as far as I could see. I found an area that I could climb onto the next ledge where I noticed a cave entrance that I couldn't see from the ground. I grabbed my headlamp and cautiously entered the cave. Once I walked into the entrance it opened up into a large cavern that went deeper into the cliff.

Sitting on a ledge was a stick under a rock pointing deeper into the cave. I ran back out to the cave entrance, looked down, and saw the two of them still lying on the ground laughing and joking around. At first, I didn't think too much about it until Lisa grabbed Jimmy's hand and held it as they continued to laugh. Thoughts entered my head that maybe Lisa liked Jimmy now. Maybe more than friends. Does that mean she doesn't like me anymore? My feelings were making me feel...well, jealous. I had never felt like that before.

Then Jimmy covered his eyes from the sun and said, "Hey, how'd you get up there?" Yep, I was spotted. Lisa quickly let go of Jimmy's hand as they both jumped up. I yelled down for them to follow the ledge to the spot where they could climb up.

Once they both reached the second ledge, I showed them the cave entrance. We all donned our headlamps and entered the cave.

They were both in just as much awe as I was. I led them over to the rock and stick pointing deeper into the cave. Jimmy said, "I don't think I want to go back there!"

"We have to if we want to help Alex!" Lisa replied.

We all looked at each other with a little fear in our eyes, took a deep breath and started heading deeper into the cave. I reminded everyone, "We have to stick together. We surely don't want to get lost in here!" As we walked deeper into the cave, the cooler it got. We stopped and we each pulled out a light jacket to help us stay warm.

After walking about twenty minutes we could hear water running up ahead. Sure enough, there was a small creek rushing across the cave. As we stood there, wondering what to do, Jimmy asked, "Do we cross this? Or do we stay here?"

"I think we have to cross," I replied.

Lisa then said, "Look guys! Another rock with a stick pointing across the creek! I guess that answers that!" She added.

I suggested, "I think we should hold hands while we cross."

"Good idea!" Jimmy replied. Once again, we took a deep breath and started to cross. Luckily, the creek was shallow, but the water was very cold.

We continued for another five minutes until we could see light and the cave opened up to the forest outside. The area was surrounded by cliffs on all sides. As we reached the edge of the cliff, we could see some fallen trees at the bottom. The three of us had to use a large vine that was growing on the side of the cliff and used it to climb down about fifteen feet to reach the bottom.

We made our way to the fallen trees and took a well-deserved break. I laid back on one of the fallen trees and gazed through the tree canopy at the blue sky above. It was very peaceful. The birds were singing and flying around like they had no care in the world. I started to think, what effect could we have on them? If any? The three of us lurched up onto our feet as we were startled. We all heard what sounded like a branch hitting a tree from above us. It was Alex! But he didn't have a branch in his hands. Alex then tilted his head back and made the same noise. He was making a noise from his throat again, not by hitting a tree with a branch. I now could tell what Lisa was thinking. She had realized the same thing. Her thoughts were, "I knew it! When everyone heard that noise, they assumed that it was made by smacking a branch against a tree. That's why nobody reports finding a broken branch in the vicinity of hearing so-called wood knocks!"

We then heard heavy thuds from all around us on the ridge that surrounded us above. It was more and more Bigfoot arriving! Five, eight, ten, twelve! Twelve plus Alex! Two of them we had already met yesterday when the saber-tooth bear chased us.

The three of us looked up with amazement at the awe of all these creatures. Just then Lisa and I could tell Jimmy was scared. Lisa reached over and held his hand. I couldn't help my thoughts. Lisa snapped her head towards me with a very surprised look on her face. She could tell that I was jealous! I had to change my thoughts immediately. I looked at Jimmy and couldn't. Lisa read my thoughts again. She scrunched her eyes at me sternly and said, "I'm just comforting Jimmy. No reason to be jealous."

Just then we picked up on Alex's thoughts, "The three of you will have plenty of time to work that out on your own. We have much more pressing issues we need to go over." Then came grunts of what seemed like laughter coming from the other Bigfoot on the ridge above. We felt a little embarrassed. Boy, I really have to be careful with my thoughts.

Alex continued, "I would like to introduce you to the rest of my family." As he did, they all made a clicking sound that we could sense as a greeting. The three of us nodded and bowed toward each of them. I knew I would never remember all their strange names. Heck, I don't even remember Alex's real name.

Alex clicked his voice and jumped with one leap from the ledge down to us. He then asked the three of us, "Can you three keep our secrets for the rest of your lives? No matter how hard it may become?"

The three of us all agreed, "Yes! Of course."

Lisa chimed in, "No one in their right mind would believe us anyway!"

"Let's hope so! My family has come far to meet with the three of you. We are hoping that your lives can make an impact for your world as well as ours," replied Alex.

"Why us kids and not adults? Or, what about leaders of all the countries around the world?" Lisa asked.

"The leaders of the world are mostly corrupt and do not have your world's best interests at heart. We usually chose children that have time, over the course of a lifetime, which can make small changes that will make a larger impact over many years."

Jimmy asked, "What do you want us to do first?"

"We need you to be more conscious of nature and the delicate balance it has on both our worlds." Alex replied. "If we're all not careful, the portals between our worlds could close forever." Alex continued, "What we both consider as Mother Earth is sensitive to changes and must be cherished. The atmosphere that surrounds the planet is also sensitive and Mother Earth will make changes to heal itself and its atmosphere. She is struggling to keep herself pure with all the types of pollution that are created by humans."

Lisa asked Alex and the others, "What can we do to help Mother Earth?"

"This is not a quick fix. Through the rest of your lives, you will live a cleaner life. Live more off the land. Grow and raise your own food.

Use less chemicals that have lasting effects upon Mother Earth and her soul and atmosphere. The largest and longer effects will come from the three of you teaching others to do the same. Some will follow and others will not. Do not focus your time on those who are not worthy of your time. Focus on those who will listen and can be taught better ways of life. Without a healthy Mother Earth...We have nothing!"

Alex concluded, "We as a species are relying on the three of you and others like you around the planet. We will contact you as we can and wish you the best in the endeavors that have been asked of you. Your lives will be much fuller as you appreciate what Mother Earth has to offer. Pass your appreciations onto your fellow humans and you will succeed."

Alex and the others all stood and bowed their heads toward us. There was an overflow of euphoric love felt though our bodies that was being sent to us from all the Bigfoot. I felt a flow of energy, emotion, and a sense of calling from them. They all then got up and disappeared into the forest and we could no longer read each other's minds.

The three of us looked at each other with amazement in our eyes. I suggested, "We all need to get going. We have a long trek to get back home."

As we headed back, conversations were not about how we had just seen a counsel of thirteen Bigfoot, something that anyone else would be in absolute shock about, something that a person would write a book about. Our conversations were on how we plan on following and implementing what was asked of us. Where do we start?

21

UNWANTED GUESTS

The three of us woke the next morning with great aspirations to make the world a better place for all. I could hear my mother talking to someone on the porch. Their conversation sounded pretty serious, so I put my shoes on and walked over to see those to whom she was talking. I peeked through the door to see two rather strange looking tall bald men dressed in black suits, hats and dark sunglasses. They were insisting to my mother on talking to everyone in the house right away. She let them know that she would have to call my father since he was already at work.

I could hear everyone else gathering in the kitchen area for breakfast. My mother asked the two strange men to wait outside and returned to the house. She then proceeded to call my father at work to explain what was happening with the two men.

Once she was off the phone Lisa's mom asked my mother, "What is going on?"

"There are two men from the government waiting outside to talk to everyone in the house. They won't even tell me why." My mother replied. My mother then went to the front door and invited the two men in. She sat them at the kitchen table and offered them coffee.

The two men shook their heads and said, "No!"

Lisa and Jimmy's mom both called their husbands and reported what was going on to them as well. All our dads were heading here to talk to these two men.

After a short wait, our dads all showed up to find out what was going on. Everyone was now sitting at the table as us three kids watched from the living room. My father asked, "Why are you two here?"

"We need to know of any strange activity on your property," one of the strange men stated.

"Like what?" My mother asked.

"Anything out of the normal," he replied.

"The only thing we can think of is that there was a black bear that was caught recently," Lisa's dad commented.

"A black bear? Around here?" The strange man asked.

"Yep, Game and Wildlife caught it and took it back to Canada where it belongs!" Jimmy's dad added.

"Anything else that may have happened? Or any other weird sightings?" The other strange man asked with a very serious face as he turned toward us. "Maybe you kids have seen something?"

The three of us must have looked in shock as he stared at us. The three of us shook our heads "No!"

The man continued to stare at us three as the other man suggested to our parents, "If you see or hear anything, be sure to let us know." The two men got up, handed my father a business card, and left in an old black Cadillac.

Our parents sat at the table and my father asked, "What on earth was that all about?"

Lisa's mom responded, "It's like they think we saw a UFO or something." Dazed and confused, our parents continued their conversations for a few minutes before everyone went back to their day.

The three of us ate our breakfast, did our chores, and met once again at the fire pit to talk about what just happened.

Jimmy opened up, "Well, that was weird."

"How do they know about us and Alex?" Lisa asked.

I said, "I don't think they know for sure that we have contact with Alex and his kind. Maybe they can detect the portal's energy or something?"

Lisa added, "Ya, and I did not like the way that the one strange man was looking at us! It was like he could read our minds!"

"Well, if he could do that, they wouldn't have had to ask us any questions, right?" Jimmy asked.

"I guess you're right!" Lisa replied. "I'm not sure why these guys would have such a problem with Alex and his kind anyway."

"They only want to help our people and our world!" I added.

"So, what do we do now?" Jimmy asked.

"We go about our normal business and start our new lives of nurturing nature," I replied.

"So, what do we want to do first, you guys?" asked Jimmy.

"I have an idea, but this will require our parents' help! But I'll need you two to back me up!" I stated.

The three of us ran inside where we found our moms finishing cleaning up from breakfast. Jimmy's mom asked, "What are you three up to?"

"Jacob has an idea for all of us and wants your help," Jimmy replied.

"What kind of help?" my mother asked.

I took a deep breath and explained, "Well, you know how much food we go through with the three families living here?"

"Yes, but this is temporary living for them, Jacob. What are you getting at?" my mother asked. Even Lisa and Jimmy at that moment had no idea what I was talking about.

I continued, "What if we built a greenhouse, here on the farm, which was big enough to grow plants year-round, for all three families?"

Jimmy's mom replied with excitement, "That's a great idea, Jacob! Think of all the vegetables we could grow!"

"Think about the money we would save!" added Lisa's mom.

My mother thought for a second and asked, "What do you think, ladies?" Jimmy and Lisa's moms both nodded their heads in agreement. My mom commented, "Now, we just need the men to build it!" The ladies laughed as Lisa, Jimmy, and I gave each other a high five on our success of the greenhouse.

We had actually succeeded in our first goal to better our living situation and our world. The first thing we wanted to do was report to Alex, but we all knew this was just the beginning.

Since our dads were all working, the three of us decided to look around the farm for supplies that we could use to help build the greenhouse with.

Behind the barn we had a shed with some used lumber in it. We found lots of boards we could use. I grabbed a couple hammers and pry bars to take out the old nails that were in some of the boards. We also found an old door and some windows that we could use.

Lisa's mom came out, found us working hard and asked, "Do you kids think you can help me down at our place really quick?"

We all said, "Sure!"

We climbed into their pickup and headed to Lisa's. She backed up to a metal building that hadn't been destroyed in the tornado. She opened the door and pulled a tarp off a pile of clear fiberglass roofing panels that would work perfectly for the greenhouse. Jimmy and I loaded the panels in the truck while Lisa and her mom went to see the progress of their new house. By the time we had loaded the truck, Lisa and her mom returned to head back to the farm.

As we were about to leave, Lisa asked, "I wonder if there is any scrap lumber in the big dumpster from the construction crew?"

"Let's check!" replied Lisa's mom.

We opened the back door of the dumpster and found all kinds of scrap lumber that we could use. We grabbed everything we could, added it to the truck and headed back.

As we drove by Jimmy's new house, I asked, "I wonder if there is more in their dumpster?"

Lisa's mom pulled the truck up and we unloaded all we could. We now had a very full truck of supplies that we could use on the greenhouse. This would save our families lots of money.

As we unloaded the truck, we discussed what kinds of vegetables we all wanted. Lisa rambled off, "Lettuce, carrots, green peppers and mushrooms."

Jimmy added his favorites, "Sweet corn, potatoes and broccoli."

"I know I don't want radishes, beets and okra!" I added.

Lisa's mom jumped into the conversation and with a big smile said, "Don't forget about strawberries and watermelons!"

The three of us all smiled in agreement and shouted, "Oh ya!" "We can't forget about those!" Lisa's added.

Once we unloaded everything, my mother had just got off the phone with my father and said, "I talked to your father, and he is excited about your idea to build a greenhouse. He said he is going to stop by the hardware store and pick up some supplies to build it." She added, "Tomorrow, we can go to town and grab all the seeds and potting soil to get started."

This all is very exciting! We are all proud for doing our part to help the planet.

22

THE GREENHOUSE

The next morning, we woke to another day of hustle and bustle in the kitchen. I was really getting used to having so many people in the house. It was the weekend, so all three of our dads didn't have to work. I sat at the breakfast table just soaking in everyone chatting about yesterday's events with the strange men visiting us. All of our parents were very confused about who they were. Are they local or from the government? Us kids felt it was best to stay out of that conversation. My mother even made the comment," I'm not even sure these two guys were even human! They were both were so pale and acted almost like robots!" The adults all gave a chuckle.

Then my father brought up the greenhouse and asked, "Are you kids ready to build that greenhouse?"

"Yes!" I responded.

Jimmy, with a mouthful of pancakes, nodded, "Yes!"

"I'm definitely ready!" Added Lisa.

"Good!" my father replied. "You kids get your chores done and then we'll get started!" he added.

The three of us hurried up and got all of our chores done and met our dads behind my mom's garden.

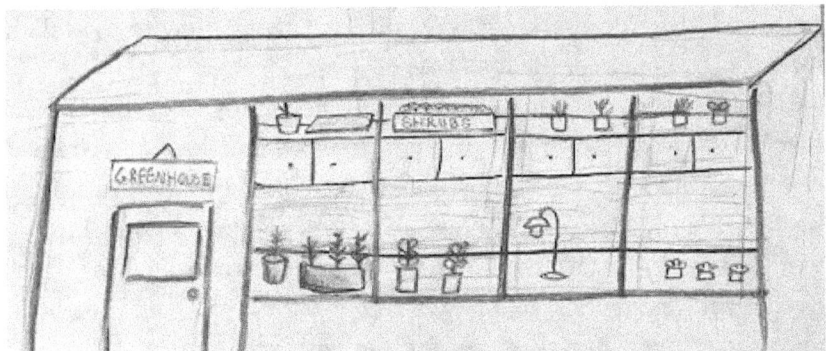

The greenhouse

My father marked out where the greenhouse was to be built. This is really going to be a team effort; all our dads, the three of us kids and our moms keeping all of us fed and hydrated. My father handed all of us kids a little tool pouch to keep a hammer, nails, and a screwdriver in. Our three dads all had their jobs to do.

My father and Lisa's dad are going to head up into the woods and cut down some pine trees for corner poles. Lisa reminded them, "For every tree we cut down, we have to plant two!"

My father thought for a second and replied, "That's a great idea, Lisa! Totally makes sense to me. I'll have the ladies run and grab a dozen baby pines to be planted."

"Have them grab some cupcakes too!" Added Jimmy. Everyone gave Jimmy a look of "What?" Jimmy smiled, held his arms out wide and said, "A hardworking man needs his fuel!" We all shook our heads and laughed as Jimmy's dad got on the tractor to scrape the ground level for the foundation of the greenhouse.

Once Jimmy's dad was done with leveling the ground, he headed up to the woods to drag down the pines that our other dads had cut up that were blown down by the tornado. Cutting down trees was not beneficial for the forest. So, using downed trees was the right thing to do for our forest. However, a downed tree was beneficial to the ecosystem of the forest. Small little bugs, beetles, grubs and many species of insects would use the fallen trees as nutrition. Smaller animals like chipmunks and squirrels would use them for shelter or a place to hide from predators. We will be leaving a few of the fallen trees for the benefit of the forest's ecosystem.

The three of us kids decided to follow Jimmy's dad up on our bikes to the woods to check out their progress. The three of us helped clear away all the branches as our dads hooked the trees up to the back of the tractor. We were just about to head down with the first load when we heard the most thunderous "Rhaaa!" come from deeper into the woods. It was so deep and loud you could feel it in your chest. We all looked at one another with fear!

My father asked, "What on earth was that?"

Jimmy's dad replied, "I don't know but it sure sounds big!"

"Well, that's not a bear. I've heard bears roar before and that was no bear!" Lisa's dad added.

My father then told everyone, "Let's get everyone back down to the farm and let the DNR (Department of Natural Resources) know about this."

We all quickly gathered everything up and headed back down to the farm. Of course, the three of us kids knew what the "Rhaaa" was but were not sure why. Was Alex upset at us? Was he warning us about possible danger? So many questions raced through our minds.

Once back down at the farm, my father called the DNR and reported the incident. They suggested that we all stay out of the woods until they stop by and investigate the situation. The three of us kids knew that we needed to find out what was going on up there.

Luckily, we were able to bring down enough logs to build the greenhouse. We also have a portable sawmill that allows us to cut boards of any size out of the trees. It also saved us lots of money and allowed us to use a renewable source. Trees are a renewable resource and as long as we replenished any trees that we used by planting new saplings then new trees would grow back. We could even plan ahead by planting trees that we were going to need in the future. This will be one of our goals from now on. Spreading this information to others would also help save both our worlds. Trees and all plant life are a terrific way to filter our atmosphere since plants breathe in CO_2

(Carbon Dioxide) from the air and release what we breathe in (Oxygen) back into the atmosphere.

Even our parents loved the idea of living off the land and not having to buy all our building supplies at a home improvement store. Plus, the end result will be growing our own vegetables, year-round, for all three of our families. Of course, the three of us kids would have to help with the upkeep of the plants. This would allow us to grow food year-round versus just the summer months from our typical outside garden. That would also mean less grocery trips to the city. Thus, saving money on gas and wear and tear on the car. Not to mention, the food would be fresher and safer for us to eat. I think this is a good start on saving both our worlds.

23

MIB ARE BACK

The next morning, I was awakened by Lisa and Jimmy standing over me. They both had a concerned look on their faces. I asked, "What's going on?"

Lisa explained, "I heard a car go by and looked out the window and saw a black Cadillac drive by and park past our fence line, just up the road."

"They must be spying on us!" Jimmy added.

"What should we do?" I asked.

Lisa replied, "I have a plan. I think we have to make them think that we know nothing, so they leave us alone."

Jimmy asked, "How do we go about making them think that?"

Lisa explained, "First of all we go about our daily business. Then hopefully if they follow us, we will take them on a wild goose chase!"

Jimmy jumped in and said, "Those weird looking guys don't look like they could keep up with us in the woods! Maybe they'll get lost, and we'll never have to deal with them ever again!"

"Wishful thinking, Jimmy!" I replied. "They are weird looking though! It's almost like they're not even human!" I added.

Lisa had a freaked out look on her face. Jimmy looked puzzled and asked, "Wait, they are human, right?"

I just shrugged my shoulders that I am unsure if they are human and headed for the dining room to eat breakfast.

You could hear Jimmy behind me commenting, "Come on! Do you guys think they might not be human, but that they might be Aliens? I don't know if I can take any more surprises, you guys."

My mother overheard Jimmy and asked, "Aliens? You kid's sure do have an active imagination. Now eat your breakfast and then get your chores done."

"Yes, mother." I replied.

The three of us once again ate breakfast quickly and headed out to do our chores. Lisa commented, "I can see the back of their car. These guys are terrible at being undercover."

"Maybe they don't care if they are seen or not." Jimmy added. "I'm sure they are watching us, so let's act normal and get our chores completed."

Men in black car

After we were done with our chores, I had an idea. I said, "Hey, guys, let's grab our bikes and head up the hill towards the woods and see if they follow us."

"That's a great idea, Jacob!" Jimmy replied.

We all grabbed our bikes and headed up the hill. I reminded them to not look back until we were over the top of the hill and out of sight. Once we were out of sight, we all dropped our bikes and crawled on our hands and knees to the top edge of the hill. We could see the whole farm from our vantage point.

"I can't see the car or the two guys," Lisa commented.

"At least you're suggesting that they are human now!" Jimmy replied. "Wait! I see movement along the fence line. It's the two men!"

"Once they get closer, we will race down the hill. Remember, we act like we don't even know that they are there." I added.

As the two men reached the edge of the woods, we took off down the hill back toward the farm. I yelled out as we reached the house, "Follow me!" I kept riding down the driveway, up the road and toward their car. We were in shock as we approached the car and drove by. The two men were in their car with the windows down and had a very confident smile on their faces. They had the look that they had duped us instead of us duping them.

We were all trying to figure out how they beat us back to their car. There was no way they could have outrun our bikes. Just then we heard a car coming down the road toward us. Was it the MIB? What do we do? Hide? From around the corner came an old farm truck. It was Mr. Tucker, a farmer who lived on the other side of the block. We waved, and he nodded and drove on by.

We rode our bikes down the road to the stop sign to discuss what had just happened. Lisa asked, "How did they beat us back to their car, Jacob?"

"I really don't think that it's possible for them to get back that quickly, unless they are capable of teleportation!" I replied.

Jimmy commented, "I agree! That would be the only way. They may be aliens, after all."

Lisa jumped into the conversation, "I'm beginning to think that anything is possible, you guys! We have Bigfoot, portals to other dimensions with dangerous beasts. Why not Aliens?"

"Let's just add Werewolves to the list, you guys!" Jimmy added.

Just then we heard a branch break in the woods behind us. We all snapped our heads to see if we could see what had made the noise. Was it the MIB? Was it Alex? The three of us were on high alert, scanning the woods for any movement.

With a high pitch crackle to his voice, Jimmy said, "We should get back to the farm where we are safer."

"I agree!" Lisa replied.

"Okay, sounds good!" I added.

On our way back we expected to have to ride by the MIB, but their car was nowhere to be seen.

"Where did they go?" Lisa asked.

"Not sure but I'm glad that they're not here," replied Jimmy.

"Let's get back to the house and research more about these MIB. I want to know what we're dealing with," Lisa added.

We raced back to the house to find the black Cadillac parked in the driveway. The three of us looked at each other with fear of what we were about to walk into.

24

MIND ERASE

The three of us entered the house very cautiously. We believed we might be in trouble for leading the MIB on a wild goose chase and wasting their time.

From the dining room we heard my mother ask, "Kids? Can you three please come in here?"

The three of us looked at each other with fear in our eyes. We all took a deep breath and entered the kitchen. Sure enough, we entered the room and the two MIB were sitting at the kitchen table. They both had a very smug look on their faces. Like they had caught us with our hand in the cookie jar.

My mother then asked us three, "Is there something that you three aren't telling us? These two men seem to think that you know more than you're telling them," she added.

The three of us looked at the men and slowly shook our heads, "No." I reluctantly asked the men, "What exactly are we talking about?"

Lisa chimed in, "Ya, what is so weird that you two were sent to spy on us?"

One of the men spoke with a slight robot voice, "We know that you kids know exactly what we are looking for. You just have to help us acquire this and we will be on our way."

My mother stated to the two men, "Unless you're going to tell us what exactly it is that you're looking for, then it's time for you two gentlemen to leave!"

The two men smiled, looked at each other and didn't budge from their seats. Then, to our surprise, the one man replied, "Okay then! We are looking for a Bigfoot that roams your woods."

My mother's mouth dropped wide open. The three of us had the look of shock on our faces as well. The cat is out of the bag now. My mother collected her thoughts and said, "There's no Bigfoot living in our woods! It's just a hermit named Alex that just wants to be left alone." My mother then asked, "Is he some sort of wanted criminal?"

"We are not interested in any hermit ma'am. We are only interested in a very dangerous Bigfoot that lives in your woods. We must capture this creature to protect everyone who lives in the area."

The second man stated, "There also may be more than one that resides in the area."

My mother looks at us three kids and asked, "Do you three know what these men are talking about?"

It wasn't like me lying but we had sworn a vow to Alex and the other Bigfoot. We knew that these Bigfoot weren't dangerous to anyone. They are very friendly and only want to work together and keep both of our worlds a wonderful place to live. So why did they want to capture Alex so badly? Maybe to study them and learn their powers. Most likely to be used as weapons against all Bigfoot or against other humans. They probably wanted to know where the portals were as well. I just knew that these two were up to no good and we shouldn't tell them a thing.

I responded to my mother with a confused face and asked, "Wait! There's possibly a Bigfoot in our woods? Holy cow! That's crazy! We have to let the hermit Alex know that it's not safe in the woods!"

"Oh dear!" My mother replied.

She started to say something about when I had hit my head and said I saw a Bigfoot but wisely Lisa cut her off and rambled off several questions toward the two men. "How do you know that there's a Bigfoot up there in the woods? Have you seen it? If you capture such a creature, what are you going to do with it?"

The two men without answering any of Lisa's questions, looked at each other again, smiled and one stood up, closed his eyes, and started talking in some language that I had never heard of before. It was like an ancient chant of some sort.

The next thing I remember is being snapped out of a deep slumber. It was my father who had just got home from work. He was asking us, "What is going on with you all?" I opened my eyes and looked around to see my mother, Lisa and Jimmy, all waking up out of a deep slumber as well. We were all groggy and were searching for our thoughts. My father once again asked, "What is going on with you guys? You were all sleeping at the table when I walked in."

My mother answered very sluggishly, "I don't know. The last thing I remember was you leaving for work."

"That was almost 9 hours ago," my father replied. "I checked the gas stove, but it was turned off," he added.

My father turned his questioning toward us three, "How about you kids, what's the last thing you can remember?"

I replied, "The last thing I remember is eating breakfast."

Lisa commented, "I don't even remember getting up this morning!"

Jimmy jumped in and said, "The last thing I remember is the two MIB sitting at the table, asking us questions."

My father blurted out, "Those two men were here again? What did they want?"

Jimmy shook his head to clear the cobwebs and said, "They were looking for something and needed our help."

"Help with what," my father asked.

"I'm not sure. That's all I remember."

My father quickly got on the phone with the local sheriff. He explained the situation and asked him to stop by.

By the time the sheriff showed up, Lisa and Jimmy's dads had both made it home as well. We all sat around the table trying to figure out what had happened.

The sheriff said, "I've looked for any government agencies that might be investigating anything in the area. So far, nothing is coming up." The sheriff ended with, "Call me as soon as possible if any of you see these two men again. Do not let them in your house."

The sheriff left, leaving us frustrated and shaking our heads with more questions than answers. The two MIB are obviously looking for Alex and the portals. The real question is, "Who do they work for and why are they here?"

25

MIB RETURN

After a long night of trying to remember what had happened yesterday, we woke to a bunch of commotion in the kitchen. Our fathers were talking about taking turns staying home. For our protection they wanted one of them to be home at all times. We all thought that this might be an innovative idea with the MIB visits. We just couldn't be careful enough. We had no idea to what extent the MIB would go to get what they wanted.

Jimmy then whispered to Lisa and me, "I remember when we were riding our bikes that a farmer named Mr. Tucker had driven by us. He had to have driven by and seen the MIB in their car."

Lisa and I didn't remember that but we were glad that Jimmy was able to remember so much. We all had different timelines that we had erased from our minds. "What do you guys say we take a ride and pay Mr. Tucker a visit then?" Lisa suggested.

"Yes, let's go now before he takes his noon nap. He does not like to be disturbed during his nap," I added.

We jumped on our bikes and took off toward Mr. Tucker's farm. We rode by Jimmy and Lisa's new homes that were almost finished. That meant that soon, it would be back to normal at my house. It made me sad knowing that they will no longer be living with us. The two of them had excitement on their faces as we rode by their new homes. I felt just the opposite.

After riding about six miles, we reached Mr. Tucker's farm. His farm was on the backside of our property. His older brother, Evan, was the previous owner of our farm. My parents bought the land after he passed away after a terrible farm accident.

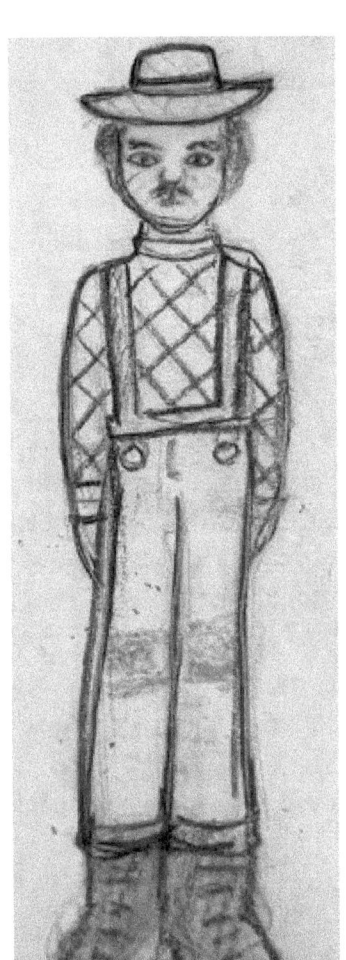

Mr. Tucker

We dismounted our bikes and stepped onto the porch. You could hear a yell from inside the house through a rickety old screen door, "Who goes there?"

"It's Jacob, Mr. Tucker!" I answered.

"Come on in, Jacob!" Mr. Tucker yelled back. We slowly opened the door and entered his house. "Hey Jacob, who do you have with you?" Mr. Tucker asked.

"My friends, Lisa and Jimmy who just moved to the neighborhood," I replied.

"You kids come on and sit down." It was dark with the only light coming from a couple of open windows. Mr. Tucker asked. "How can I help you kids?"

"Well, do you remember seeing us yesterday on our bikes?" I asked.

"Oh, yes, I do. I was on my way into town to get some more feed for the horses," Mr. Tucker replied.

"Ok, cool!" I replied. "Did you happen to see a black Cadillac parked on the side of the road near our house?" I asked.

Immediately, Mr. Tucker stood up and with a very serious look on his face asked, "You kids are seeing an old black Cadillac?"

Lisa replied. "Yes, with two weird, bald men dressed in black suits asking a lot of questions."

"Oh dear. They're back!" Replied Mr. Tucker.

"What do you mean, they're back?" I asked with concern.

Mr Tucker struggled for something to say, or not say, before asking, "You know my brother used to live on your farm before you guys did, right?"

"Yes, I knew that," I replied.

Mr Tucker then started to explain, "Ok, how do I tell you this? Oh heck, I'll just tell you kids straight. My brother told me that he had a friend that lived in the woods."

Lisa interrupted him, "Let me guess, his friend was a Bigfoot?"

With surprise on his face, Mr. Tucker continued, "Umm, yes! He said it was Bigfoot. Actually, several of them." He added. "They would talk to him but not actually talk with words. You know, in your head!"

Lisa commented, "Yes, they talk to us telepathically as well! Plus, they want us to help them protect our world and that will in turn help their world."

"Oh, ya! They travel through portals between their world and ours," Lisa added.

"Oh wow! I guess my brother wasn't crazy after all!" replied Mr. Tucker. Mr. Tucker paced back and forth before suddenly stopping to ask, "Can I meet them?"

The three of us looked at each other and shrugged our shoulders. I wasn't sure that they would like that. They trusted us but bringing him to Alex might break our trust. We may lose our ability to see Alex if we make the wrong choice.

After deliberating with Lisa and Jimmy and thinking about it for a minute, we decided we would try to include Mr. Tucker and try to let him meet Alex. "No promises, Mr. Tucker," I announced.

"Ya, and you must do one thing before we can take you to meet with Alex," Lisa added.

"Anything! What do you need from me?" replied Mr. Tucker.

Jimmy announced, "You have to pinky swear that no matter what, you can never tell anyone, especially the MIB about Alex or the portals."

Mr Tucker jumped up from his chair, stuck out his pinky towards us and said, "I pinky swear to never tell anyone about Alex and the portals!"

The three of us looked at each other in acceptance and joined our pinky fingers with Mr. Tucker to seal the promise.

"Now what?" asked Mr. Tucker.

"I think tomorrow morning after our chores, we go to find Alex," I replied.

"Sounds perfect! I'll see you there in the morning," replied Mr. Tucker with excitement in his voice.

26

FINDING ALEX

The next morning, we woke, gobbled down our breakfast and rushed off to get our chores done. We once again gathered some supplies and treats for Alex. The three of us were kind of worried that Alex may think that we betrayed him by bringing Mr. Tucker with us. We had already surprised him with Jimmy.

We were waiting on the porch when Mr. Tucker drove up in his old pickup truck. My mother was just leaving for the dress shop and asked, "Why is Mr. Tucker here?"

I had to think quickly. As hard as it is, I obviously couldn't tell her the truth. Lisa stood up and responded, "Mr. Tucker wanted to show us a special spot in the woods that he and his brother would hang out at when they were kids."

"Oh, that's very nice of you, Mr. Tucker," my mother replied. "I'm also glad to have an adult with the kids. Every time we turn around there's a wild animal or people causing havoc!" she added.

Mr. Tucker smiled and replied, "It's no problem, ma'am. I am looking forward to our adventure and maybe reliving some old memories that my brother and I shared many years ago."

Mr. Tucker and the kids

Once my mother left, we threw our supplies into the back of Mr. Tucker's truck, jumped into the cab and headed up the trail to the woods. Mr. Tucker commented in a slight emotional tone, "It's been many years since I've driven up this trail. My brother always would tell me that these woods are very special. I didn't really understand what he meant until now."

Lisa touched Mr. Tucker shoulder and said with compassion, "You now can hopefully be a part of your brother's life by meeting with Alex, who once knew your brother."

While wiping a tear that was running down his face, he said "That would be great, you guys. Thank you for including me."

We knew by Mr. Tucker's emotions, that we had made the right choice to bring him along. This was hopefully a time that he could bond with his long-lost brother. Just driving up here we could all tell that he was thinking about his brother and all the moments they had shared. Mr Tucker told us a few stories about his brother on the drive. It was nice to see that they were close and that he missed his brother.

Mr. Tucker drove us as far as he could in his truck. "I guess this is end of the road, kids," he announced. We all jumped out of the truck and grabbed our backpacks.

I suggested, "If you, Mr. Tucker, could bring up the rear so that when we reach Alex he won't be alarmed."

"That's a good idea, Jacob," replied Lisa. "We don't want to scare Alex off before we can explain Mr. Tucker's presence."

We walked for quite a while through the woods. Mr. Tucker spoke up and said, "Hey, I think we are getting close, kids."

We all stopped, and I asked him, "You can sense Alex?"

"No, but we are almost to the large ravine that my brother and I would hang out at. It's where he confided in me about seeing a Bigfoot." Mr Tucker added, "All I did was pick on him and tell him that he was crazy after telling me his secret." We could tell in his voice that he now regrets what he had said to his brother. We understood though. It's not every day that someone tells you a fantastic tale of a friendly monster that lives in your woods!

Within fifteen minutes we had reached the edge of the ravine. Mr. Tucker commented, "Right there by that rock was where my brother and I would sit. I think he wanted to tell me about seeing Bigfoot much earlier in our lives."

"What makes you think that, Mr. Tucker?" Lisa asked.

"Well, we had been coming to this spot for a couple years before he confided in me about his Bigfoot experience," Mr. Tucker replied.

Jimmy patted Mr. Tucker on his back and stated, "Wow! Your brother must have known about these creatures and wanted to include you as part of the secret." Jimmy added, "Even though you didn't believe him back then, now is your chance to rectify his trust in you."

Mr. Tucker just nodded his head, took a deep breath, and sat on the rock that he and his brother sat on all those years ago. We just let him sit there for a few minutes in silence. We could tell that he was struggling with his emotions and memories.

After scanning the ravine for Alex, Lisa suggested, "Why don't we head down to the creek at the bottom and see if there are any signs of Alex around."

Mr. Tucker stood up and said, "That sounds great, you guys. It sure would be nice to meet this, Alex." We grabbed our things and headed down to the bottom of the ravine.

We all searched along the bottom of the ravine for any signs of

Alex or the portal, but with no luck. I commented, "Maybe we should get heading back."

"Just a little longer, Jacob. He's gotta be around," Lisa replied optimistically.

Suddenly, Mr. Tucker, who was off on his own just down the creek yelled out, "Hey kids! Come here! Quick!" The three of us ran over to Mr. Tucker to find him having a conversation with himself. Mr. Tucker was saying, "I do! I do believe!" It was then the three of us were sensing what Mr. Tucker was. It was Alex! He was telepathically speaking with Mr. Tucker.

Alex then asked Mr. Tucker, "Can I trust you?"

"Yes! You can trust me!" replied Mr. Tucker.

The three of us kids all replied to Alex, "You can trust him, Alex! Mr. Tucker pinky swore that he will never divulge anything about your kind, your world or about the portals."

Alex stepped out from behind a large oak tree that must have been at least two hundred years old and approached us. Seeing Alex was still shocking for us but for Mr. Tucker, it had to have been much more. Alex and Mr. Tucker just stood there for a moment, taking each other in.

Alex took a deep breath and confirmed to Mr. Tucker, "Yes, Finn, I knew your brother Bud. He was very special to us and lived his life with us always in mind. We were very sad to find that he was no longer with us. We were lucky enough to have these three to take over Bud's appreciation for our species," Alex added.

"I would love to help and hopefully fill a portion of my brother's shoes. I owe that to my brother," replied Mr. Tucker.

The touching meeting of Alex and Mr. Tucker really made me think how precious our lives are. It can all be taken away in the blink of an eye. I glanced at Lisa to see tears in her eyes that she was trying unsuccessfully to hide. I walked over to her, gave her a big hug and said, "I'm so glad you're in my life!"

It must have been uncomfortable for her since she squiggled out of my hug and as she stepped back stated, "Thanks, Jacob, but now's not the time to be flirting."

I was dumbfounded. "I wasn't flirting!" I replied.

Lisa gave me a weird, frustrated face and asked Alex, "Can I ask you a few questions?"

"Of course, you can," replied Alex.

Lisa moved over and sat on the big rock near Alex. Jimmy and I followed and sat on the rock next to Lisa. As Lisa started asking her first question, you could hear Mr. Tucker say, "Wow! I'm going to have to get used to this!"

Lisa commented, "Yes, so try not to talk while someone else is talking."

Mr. Tucker put his hands up and said, "Sorry, it won't happen again."

Lisa continued with her question to Alex, "So, why did you yell really loud when we were cutting wood with our parents for our greenhouse?"

Alex moved over and sat on the grass across from us and replied, "I needed to scare you all out of the woods before someone ended up in the portal." Alex added, "You were all way too close!"

Jimmy nervously jumped up and added, "Ya, I do not recommend that anyone ever go to Alex's world. There are big dangerous monsters, which are definitely not friendly over there."

Mr. Tucker chimed in, "Well, I surely don't want to run into those monsters!"

"No, you don't!" added Jimmy.

I responded to Alex, "Well, that's good to know. We just wanted to be sure."

Lisa continued with her questions for Alex, "Why is it that no one can take a good picture of your species?"

Alex took a deep breath and explained, "If you know about energy, of all things, then you might understand the vibration of all things. Everything vibrates at its own frequency. Take that rock, for instance. It is very solid and vibrates at a lower frequency. The trees vibrate at a slightly higher frequency. You, as humans, vibrate higher and we, as you call us Bigfoot, vibrate at a much higher frequency.

The camera has a tough time picking up our frequency as being a solid object. That is why your photos are always blurry."

Lisa, in wonderment replied, "Wow! Now we just need to create a camera that can capture your higher frequencies!"

Jimmy jumped into the conversation, "Ya, then we can prove that you really exist!"

Alex gave a gruff growl that set Jimmy back and stated, "Jimmy, if I remember right, the goal is not to prove our existence."

Jimmy responded nervously, "Oh ya, I knew that! I mean, I would never!"

Lisa smacked the back of Jimmy's head to let him know that he's said too much.

Lisa stood up and said, "I have one more question, Alex."

Alex nodded to Lisa in approval. Lisa started out, "Ok, this one may be a little more personal. Do you have, like, feelings like we humans do?"

Alex gave a short grunting laugh, leaned back, and answered, "Yes, we care for ourselves, our families and others. We even have compassion, hope, sadness, fear, and anger. We are very similar as humans when it comes to emotions. Yet, we are also very different. We don't have what you call civilizations. We would be more like your native species. We have always lived off land and water as our ancestors did. There is no cultivation of crops or raising of domesticated animals for food. There are no writings of our history. It has always been orally passed down from generation to generation."

Lisa smiled and responded, "Your species is just like our past in so many ways. That is before we thought that we needed to conquer Mother Earth, instead of living in harmony with her."

Alex walked over to Lisa, looked her straight in the eyes and stated, "You are very insightful. Your life's mission is to pass your knowledge off to others so that Mother Earth can continue to survive."

"But how do I do that, Alex?" Lisa asked.

"You all are smart and caring people. That is why we have accepted you as our ambassadors of the cause that we hold sacred. When the time comes, you will know what to do," Alex replied and continued, "I must go for now. We will be expecting great things from the four of you." Alex reached out his long arms and handed each one of us a crystal rock.

"Wow, these are beautiful!" Lisa excitedly blurted out!"

Alex then let us know why he gave us the crystals, "These crystals are very special and are from my world. I have the four matching crystals from your world. They will help us communicate telepathically. Even when we are in our own world, we will be able to unconsciously know what each other is thinking. They must be kept with you at all times for them to work. The longer you do so the more powerful they become. In time, we will communicate as if we are standing next to each other, as we are now."

With a big smile on her face, Lisa announced, "I will make them into necklaces for all of us to wear."

"That's a great idea, Lisa," replied Alex as he turned and gave a loud whoop.

We watched as Alex walked away back into the woods. Jimmy took a deep breath, stretched, and said, "I guess we had better get back before dark, you guys."

Mr. Tucker replied, "Yes, let's get going. I'm sure we all have chores to do."

As we walked back to the truck, Mr. Tucker talked about his brother, Bud. It was just as Alex explained. Mr. Tucker was passing down oral stories from his past. We realized that today, Mr. Tucker and his brother were now back together.

27

JACOB HAS AN IDEA

I lay awake that night just thinking of what Alex had said about Mother Earth being sacred. Living off the land like our early ancestors had lived for thousands of years. I wondered how we could influence as many people as possible in our lifetimes to help make a difference to both Alex's and our worlds. This was quite a daunting task for the four of us. Sure, it would be a lot of work, but it would make a slight difference if our four families could achieve this. However, to really make a difference, we would need the entire world to follow our lead. The four of us would need to brainstorm to find the right path to success. We have to keep in mind that we have our whole lives to achieve this, but we would need to get started right away.

As I laid there thinking, Lisa started to stir. I quietly asked, "Hey, Lisa, are you awake?" There was no response. I asked again a little louder, "Hey, are you awake?"

"I am now!" Lisa replied with a little grumpiness to her voice.

I asked Lisa, "Would you talk to me about what steps we should take next?"

"Steps for what?" She replied.

"Steps that Alex wants us to take to help Mother Earth," I replied.

Mud bricks

Lisa rolled over, looked at me and said, "Go to sleep, Jacob! We can discuss this in the morning."

"Okay, I'm sorry. That sounds good," I replied as Lisa started to snore.

From the other side of the room, I heard a chuckle. It was Jimmy. I softly asked Jimmy, "What are you laughing at?"

He chuckled again and replied, "Lisa snores like a freight train." We both gave a laugh. Lisa then snorted as we had disturbed her sleep once again. Jimmy and I couldn't help it and laughed louder.

Lisa sat up, looked at Jimmy and I with distain in her eyes and asked, "What is wrong with you two?" Jimmy and tried to hold it in but burst out in laughter. Lisa rolled her eyes, laid back down, pulled her pillow over her face and gave a scream, "Ahhhh, boys!" As Jimmy and I once again laughed, Lisa started to laugh as well with us.

Lisa stood up, walked over to the counter in the kitchen, and grabbed a pen and paper. She then proceeded to sweep my legs off the couch and said, "Ok, let's brainstorm and make a list of what we think would be things that we might want to achieve. Then we can make a plan that would actually accomplish those goals."

"That's a great idea!" Jimmy responded as he sat down with us.

"So, where do we start though?" I asked.

Lisa replied, "Let's just put ideas to paper and we can work them out as the next step. Then whatever makes the most sense will be what we work on first."

"You know, you're pretty smart. So, why don't you go first, Lisa," Jimmy stated.

Lisa thought for a second and suggested, "We have the greenhouse already so why don't we focus on a natural product that can be used for building greenhouses?"

"A recycled product like plastics?" I asked.

"Maybe," Lisa replied.

"What about bricks that are made out of mud and not cement?" Jimmy responded.

"You mean like our ancestors would have done, right?" I asked in agreement.

"Yep, just like that!" Jimmy replied.

Lisa chimed in, "All we need to do is get the recipe to make them!"

"Recipe? We're not baking a cake!" Jimmy replied.

We all laughed at one another until Lisa said in a serious tone, "We now have one idea. I'm tired and you both know what's it's like if I don't get my beauty sleep!"

Jimmy and I laughed some more as Lisa shook her head in disapproval. The three of us finally laid back down to go to sleep. I knew that from tomorrow on, we will be working on protecting Mother Earth.

28

SAVING MOTHER EARTH

The three of us woke up a little sluggish for breakfast due to having been up part of the night brainstorming on how we should start doing our part of protecting Mother Earth. We know that society as a whole has been all about living as easily and comfortably as possible. Thus, using disposable products is short lived and we just end up throwing them away when they break, or the latest model comes around. All these disposable products have been filling up landfills for at least the last seventy-five years. Many products have to be produced by creating large factories that pollute the land when mined. That takes large machinery and lots of fuel to run such machinery. And of course, a large factory is needed to make the products in. These factories pollute our air and waterways negatively. This is harmful to all living plants and creatures. Including humans. It all just seems like such a waste.

Technology kept popping up in my head as we spoke to Alex yesterday. I think I understand now that Alex was subtly hinting that many forms of technology can be bad for the planet. There are so many chemicals that are harmful to the environment as well. All a result of technologies that we use to speed up plant and animal growth for food products. I felt that there are so many things we could work on throughout our lives. Our task to help save the planet is going to be very daunting. I remember my mother and father talking about how politics, governments, and greed dictate what happens around the planet. So, to change this way of life will be an uphill battle.

What we want to do is keep everything we do from now on to natural, renewable products that don't require harming our beautiful planet.

Once we finished our breakfast and daily chores, the three of us sat down at the fire pit to discuss our plans on how to go about making these bricks.

Lisa spoke up and announced, "I've been searching on how to make these mud bricks. We only need clay or silty soil, straw, and water. You just mix together and put them into forms, pop them out and lay them in the sun to dry. That's it!"

I replied, "That's easy enough! I can make the forms from some scrap wood and there's straw we can use from the barn. Plus, at the bottom of the field is where all the runoff from the fields collects. There's gotta be lots of clay there."

Jimmy asked, "Can we use the tractor to dig up the clay?"

"Nope! We use shovels and the wheelbarrow," Lisa replied. "Remember, we want to do this without machinery that pollutes our air," she added.

Jimmy replied, "Oh ya, you're right. It would be so much easier if we used the tractor though."

"Jimmy! No! We can't think like that! That's the problem with the world today!" Lisa snapped back.

Jimmy put up his hands as to give up and said, "Okay, I get it!"

Lisa said, "Okay. Now that we have that settled, let's go inform Mr. Tucker about our plan."

We jumped on our bikes and tore off down the road. As we neared Jimmy's new house, we saw Jimmy's dad waving to us to stop. We pulled up and Jimmy's dad said with a big smile on his face, "Hi kids! Lisa and Jimmy, you both will be glad to know that both our houses will be done and ready to move into by early next week. Just in time for school!"

Jimmy yelled out in excitement, "That's awesome, dad!"

Lisa, with a big smile on her face and slight tear in her eye, replied, "Yes, I can't wait to have my own room and some privacy once again."

Lisa and Jimmy were very happy about the news, but I started to feel sad that what I had thought of us as one big family would now be just myself and my parents once again. I enjoyed the liveliness of our three families under one roof. You never knew what was going to happen next. We all have had so much happen to of us this summer. It definitely will be a summer to remember. I also appreciated their help with my chores. It gave us time to have our adventures in the woods and with Alex. Jimmy, Lisa and I have definitely become best friends, and I wouldn't change a thing that we did this summer.

I then noticed that Lisa was shaking my shoulder and asking, "Hey, are you alright?"

I collected my thoughts and since I didn't want to pour my feeling out, I just replied, "Ya, I just can't believe school starts in a couple weeks!" I added, "Not that I don't like school but I'm not ready to go back!"

Lisa responded, "Ya, I get it! We had so much fun this summer. There were a few bumps in the road, but we all came out just fine!"

"For sure! We got to bring in a new friend too!" I said as I smiled and nodded towards Jimmy.

Jimmy chimed in, "I bet that none of the kids at school had a crazy summer like ours!"

The three of us laughed and took off on our bikes towards Mr. Tucker's farm. We were stopped in our tracks as we turned the corner and saw the old black Cadillac parked in Mr. Tucker's driveway, "What should we do?" I asked.

"Let's go see what's going on!" Lisa replied.

As Jimmy started to turn his bike around to go back home, he replied, "No way! Those guys scare me!"

Lisa lashed out at Jimmy, "Don't be a chicken! Mr. Tucker may need our help!"

"Fine, but I'm leaving the first sign of danger!" Jimmy replied.

We nervously rode up to the front door of Mr. Tucker's house and parked our bikes. We looked at each other, took a deep breath, and knocked on the door. There was no answer. I knocked again and announced, "Hey Mr. Tucker! It's Jacob!" Still no answer. We began to worry. Where could he be?

Lisa said, "Let's check out by the barn." Jimmy and I agreed, and we headed out back. Once we were closer, we could hear talking coming from the barn. We continued to the open barn doors. As we peered in, we could see the backs of the two MIB.

Mr. Tucker was telling them "You two must be crazy! I've never heard of anyone seeing a Bigfoot on that farm or anywhere near here."

I decided to go in and help break up this meeting. Lisa and Jimmy followed close behind. I spoke up and said, "Hey, Mr. Tucker! Oh, I see you've met these two."

Mr. Tucker smiled and replied, "Yes, I have, unfortunately. They think that there's a Bigfoot on your farm."

"Wow! That's crazy!" I replied.

"They also think my brother knew of them too!" Mr. Tucker added.

The two MIB seemed frustrated by our arrival. One of them announced in his robotic voice, "Our business is done here." They both glared at us as they walked by and headed for their car.

We waited for them to drive away before saying anything further to each other. Once they pulled away, I said, "Enough about them!" We all laughed.

Lisa asked, "Mr. Tucker, do you know how to make mud bricks?"

"Mud bricks?" He asked.

"Yes, we've decided to make natural mud bricks to use instead of building materials to finish our Greenhouse and any other buildings we may need," Lisa replied.

Mr. Tucker's face lit up and he said, "That's a great idea, kids.

We're going back to primitive man to help get folks back to basics." He added, "I love the idea!"

"Keeping the four of us busy making bricks will hopefully keep those MIB off Alex's trail," Lisa commented.

Mr. Tucker with pride in his voice suggested, "Let's get all the supplies we need and meet tomorrow, after morning chores at your place, Jacob." The three of us agreed and headed home to get everything ready. Tomorrow will begin our next adventure to help save Mother Earth!

29

MOTHER EARTH SPEAKS

The next morning, we woke excitedly that today we would start making all natural mud bricks. As the three of us ate our breakfast as fast as we possibly could, my mother asked, "Hey, what's the big rush, kids?"

"After our chores are done, Mr. Tucker is going to meet us here to show us how to make mud bricks," I replied.

My mother with pride in her voice said, "I think what you kids are doing is great!"

The three of us replied, "Thanks!"

We rushed through our morning chores, which were going to be just mine, once again, within a couple weeks. I wasn't looking forward to that. I was already sad and regrettably counting down the days of not having my extended family around.

Right after our chores were done, Lisa ran into the house yelling, "I'll be right back!" Jimmy and I looked at each other and shrugged our shoulders. A few minutes later she emerged with a pair scissors and some string.

Until Mr. Tucker arrives, the three of us sat down by the fire pit to go over our plan of building mud bricks. Lisa asked Jimmy and I for our crystals that were given to us by Alex. She laid them together on a stump. A weird sensation came over us. It was almost the same sensation when we were near Alex. We could sense each other's thoughts without speaking a word. The crystals seemed to be emitting a slight glow. It was almost like someone had turned on a switch to power them up.

Lisa tied a string around each one, turning them into a necklace that we can wear around our necks.

Jimmy stood up and asked, "Hey, do you guys hear that?"

"Hear what?" I replied.

Jimmy put his finger to his mouth to quiet us and said, "It's Mr. Tucker."

Lisa and I both stood up and listened for a second before I asked, "You are telepathically speaking with him?"

Jimmy laughed and said, "No! I can hear his truck coming up the road."

Lisa and I looked at each other with a questioning expression on our faces as we turned our heads to get a better listen. Then, out of the blue, we both could also hear Mr. Tucker's old pickup truck heading our way.

Mr. Tucker pulled into the driveway with a big smile on his face and yelled out the window, "Hey kids! Are we ready to help save Mother Earth?"

The three of us smiled, put our arms in the air and yelled out, "Yes!" We were all very excited to get started. We all knew that making mud bricks isn't the answer to solve all of Mother Earth's problems but it's only the beginning.

Mr. Tucker stepped out of his truck and opened the back tailgate. He had brought a can of old rusty nails and old boards that we could use to build brick forms.

Lisa piped up and asked Mr. Tucker, "Do you have your crystal with you?"

"I sure do," replied Mr. Tucker as he reached into his pocket and handed it to Lisa.

"I'll make a necklace for you, just like ours," Lisa stated.

"While you make his necklace, we can start making forms to make the bricks," I suggested.

"Well, let's get started then boys!" Mr. Tucker said to Jimmy and me as he grabbed the supplies out of the back of his truck.

We would only need a couple forms. Once you filled the form, you would then dump out the brick and lay it out to dry in the sun. Once they are dry, they can be stacked and are ready to use. We measured, cut the boards, and nailed them together. Now all we need is to get all the supplies to make the bricks.

We gathered up a couple of bails of straw and loaded them into the back of Mr. Tucker's truck. I grabbed a few old five-gallon buckets and filled them with water. The last ingredient we would need would be the clay, which had built up over many years, at the bottom of the field.

"Okay everyone. Time to load up and get to making some bricks!" Mr. Tucker stated. We all squeezed into the front seat and headed to the bottom of the field.

"This looks like a good spot," announced Mr. Tucker as we pulled up near the soft, slightly muddy area. We all piled out of the truck with excitement to finally get started.

As we unloaded all of our tools and supplies, Lisa suggested, "Maybe we should have a ritual before we start!"

"That's a great idea! What do you have in mind?" I replied.

"I know," Jimmy blurted out, "Let's put our crystals together and thank Mother Earth for her generosity."

"That's a great idea!" added Mr. Tucker.

The four of us stood face to face and touched our crystals that Alex had given us together. When we did, they all started to light up.

Lisa commented, "Wow! This is so awesome!"

Jimmy spoke up with surprise and said, "I think I can read everyone's mind right now!"

"I think you're right, Jimmy!" I replied in a little disbelief.

Mr. Tucker shook his head in agreement and replied, "I feel like I can feel my brother with us as well!" His eyes started to tear up a little and he asked, "Would you mind if I give thanks to Mother Earth?" The three of us nodded our heads in agreement.

Mr. Tucker cleared his throat and said, "Dear Mother Earth, with all your power, we would like to help maintain your grandeur. We thank you for all you give and promise to do our best to utilize your resources responsibly."

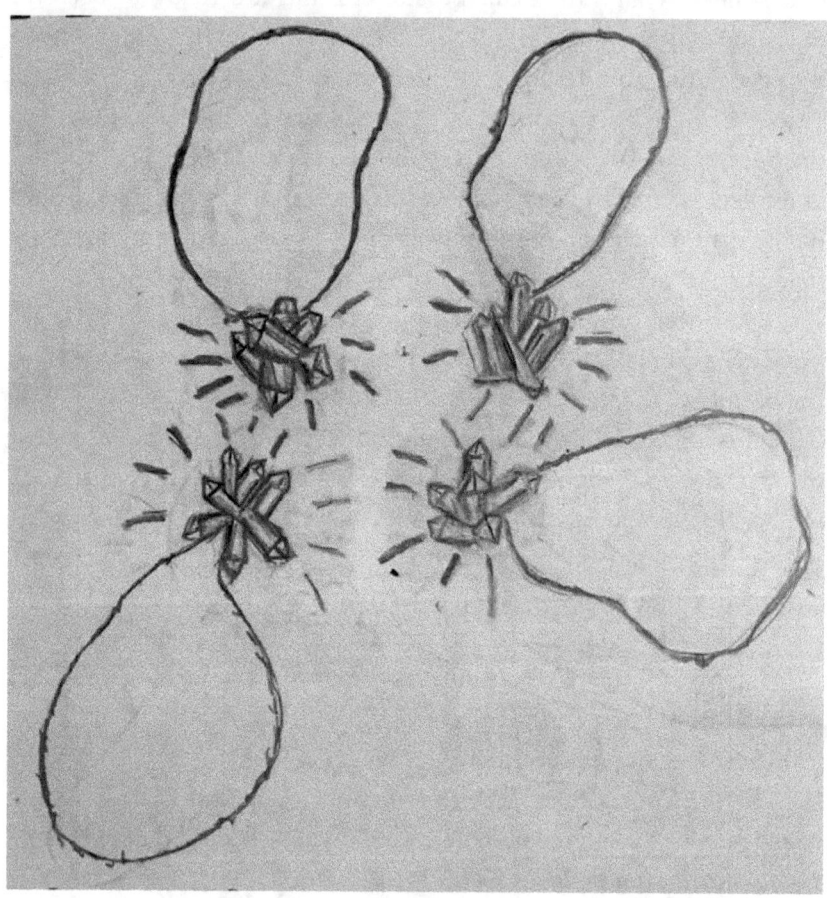

The four crystals

We all stood there, still holding our crystals together for a few seconds, with our eyes closed. Suddenly we all heard inside our heads, "You have all been chosen and your efforts will not be in vain. Follow your hearts and all that is, will be answered."

At that instant we all let go of the crystals and took a step back. We all felt as though we had just woken from a dream. We were all in disbelief and weren't even sure if that really happened.

Lisa just started saying, "Wow! Wow! Wow! Did we just connect with Mother Earth?"

"I believe we did!" replied Mr. Tucker. "How many people can say that?" Mr. Tucker continued.

We were all just standing there in shock when we heard a knock from the edge of the woods. Lisa's eyes got big and stated, "That's got to be Alex!"

Sure enough, Alex began talking telepathically, "You have all impressed me. It is seldom that humans are able to get a reply from Mother Earth." Alex added, "You are all heading in the right direction."

We all gave a quick, "Thanks!"

Alex then directed his conversation towards Mr. Tucker, "I have a special gift that will give you some insight. Please join me at the ravine tomorrow. You all are welcome to join."

"Of course! We all will be there," Mr. Tucker replied.

And, just like that Alex was gone.

Lisa asked Mr. Tucker, "What do you think Alex means about giving you some insight?"

"Not sure, Lisa," replied Mr. Tucker.

Jimmy chimed in, "Well, it must be a good thing, since Alex said it was a special gift."

Mr. Tucker looked around, grabbed a shovel, and said, "We had better get busy!" We all smiled, grabbed a shovel, and started digging for clay.

30

SPECIAL GIFT

The next morning, we woke, ate a delicious breakfast our mothers had prepared and got our chores done. By the time we had everything done Mr. Tucker was driving up to meet us. You can tell that Mr. Tucker was very excited to see Alex again and to find out what his special gift was going to be.

We all piled into Mr. Tucker's truck and headed up the trail once again to the ravine. Mr. Tucker took a detour past the bricks we made yesterday. They all looked great and were drying nicely. It was a lot of work to make the bricks, but the reward would be the feeling of pride and accomplishment. Our goal is to make and use natural homemade products as much as possible. My father said that one of our projects may be good enough to turn into an actual business. Any money we made could be put back into our efforts. We would have to be disciplined and change our lifestyle to fit our goals.

The second part of our goal would be to share our knowledge with others in hopes that they would follow. Making the process enjoyable and effective would be the best way to influence others and have them join in. Every little bit would help the cause.

We then headed up into the woods toward the ravine. We were all very curious about the special gift Alex was talking about. Mr. Tucker drove us as far as the trail could take us. Once again, we would need to walk the rest of the way. As we walked Mr. Tucker asked us three, "Hey kids, what could Alex be talking about?"

Jimmy gave a little chuckle and said, "Maybe Alex has a girlfriend for you!" We all laughed out loud.

Mr. Tucker needed to laugh because he had been very nervous since Alex mentioned the surprise yesterday. None of us has any idea of what to expect.

Suddenly Mr. Tucker spun around and asked Lisa with a snippy attitude, "What do you mean that Alex's surprise might not be a good thing?"

"I didn't say anything!" Lisa snapped back.

"Ya, well, you're thinking it!" Mr. Tucker replied.

We then realized that we must be close to Alex. We were reading each other's minds, telepathically.

Lisa spoke up and said, "Sorry, Mr. Tucker. I'm sure it's going to be something wonderful."

"I sure hope so," replied Mr. Tucker. "Now, let's find Alex and get this over with," he added.

We slowly made our way down the rocky trail to the bottom of the ravine. Out of nowhere, Lisa gave out a loud, "Whoop!" She had definitely caught us all off guard.

"What on earth are you doing?" I asked.

"I'm calling for Alex so that he knows we are here," Lisa replied.

"Couldn't you have done that telepathically?" Jimmy asked.

With a shoulder shrug and a big smile, Lisa replied, "What's the fun in that?"

We all just shook our heads and waited for Alex. While we waited, Mr. Tucker paced nervously back and forth. Before you know it, Alex came out from behind the large pine trees that lined the creek.

Alex greeted us with a loud, "Cluck!" A noise that everyone thinks is banging a large stick against a tree, calling them tree knocks. However, the noise is made with their tongue and throat.

Alex walked right up to Mr. Tucker, put his large hand onto his shoulder and said, "Today is going to be a very special day for you. If you're willing?"

Mr. Tucker with slight fear, slowly replied, "Yes, yes I'm willing."

Alex explained more to Mr. Tucker, "This is going to be very emotional, and I need you to prepare yourself for that."

Mr. Tucker now looked even more scared but asked, "What exactly is going to happen? You had said this was going to be a special event," Mr. Tucker continued.

Alex patted Mr. Tucker on the back and replied, "I'm about to show something that may shock you and I just need you to be strong."

"Okay, I am prepared for whatever you have for me," Mr. Tucker replied.

Alex put his huge hand on top of Mr. Tucker's head and asked him to close his eyes and clear his mind.

Mr. Tucker did as Alex instructed. Alex directed his attention to us three kids and asked, "Now you three close your eyes and focus on Mr. Tucker." We all did as Alex instructed.

After a few moments we started seeing, in our mind, flashes of light that gradually turned into short bursts of reality. We could see the trees that surrounded us. Then we started seeing a person walking toward us. I don't know who this person is.

Mr. Tucker suddenly said telepathically with a lot of emotion that we all could feel, "It's Bud! My brother Bud!" Mr. Tucker couldn't believe what he was seeing.

We were all watching this as if it were live. This was a memory of Alex's with Mr. Tucker's brother, Bud. All of us continued to watch Alex's memory play out. Mr. Tucker's brother, Bud, smiled and said, "Well, I told my brother Finn about you. He thinks I'm crazy. I'm sure that someday he will come around," Bud continued.

Alex replied to Bud, "Hopefully your brother will be ready to join you in your endeavors to help your and our worlds."

Bud replied, "There is nothing I would rather do than work together with my brother."

We all could tell that seeing and hearing his brother Bud was really affecting Mr. Tucker. The last thing we saw and heard was Bud telling Alex, "I'll eventually get Finn on board, you'll see!"

Then we all opened our eyes to see Mr. Tucker on his knees, sobbing. We all could feel his emotions. With tears in our eyes, we ran over and hugged him to show our support.

After a couple minutes, Mr. Tucker announced, "I'm okay guys. I just need to sit for a bit."

"That had to have been a lot to take in," replied Lisa. Mr. Tucker nodded while nervously running his hands through his hair.

Jimmy and I grabbed a few logs for us to sit on. Alex just sat up against a large tree and quietly studied Mr. Tucker.

"Thank you for showing me your memory of my brother, Alex. I don't know how to ever repay you." Mr. Tucker announced.

"It was my pleasure. Your gratitude is all that is needed," replied Alex.

"I could tell that my brother really appreciated and enjoyed your friendship," said Mr. Tucker.

"Yes, and I enjoyed being his friend. Just as I'm enjoying being friends with the four of you," replied Alex.

Alex stood up and said, "Just like Mr. Tucker's brother Bud, there have been many who we have communicated with throughout time. Now we are collaborating with you four and many around the world. We hope to continue this partnership with those we trust in the future. There are those whose curiosity is harmful to our cause."

Lisa spoke up, "You mean like the Men In Black that have followed us? Not to mention erasing our memory."

"Yes!" Alex replied. Alex explained more about the MIB, "They are very powerful creatures that want to control everyone and everything."

"Wait!" I said and continued, "You said creatures? Are you saying that they are not human?"

Alex scratched his head and explained, "These, Men In Black are not from either of our worlds. They are shape shifting Lizard beings that live in inner earth."

Jimmy fell back to the ground and with both hands over his head yelled out, "What? Now we find out that there is Lizard people, and they live inside the earth?" Jimmy continued, "I don't know how much more I can take, you guys!"

We were all now shaking our heads in disbelief of the news Alex has just announced. I felt like I was in a dream.

Alex explained more, "Don't worry, these Lizard people will not harm you. You have no special powers like we and the Lizard people do. They are just curious about humans. However, they would love to get their hands on my species to see if they could harness our abilities to add to their own. That would make them even more powerful. We are afraid that they would eventually try to takeover our world and make it theirs."

Lisa asked Alex, "So why don't they want to take over our world?"

"Your sun is too bright for their sensitive skin and eyes. That is why they wear sunglasses all the time." Alex replied and continued, "Our world is much dimmer than yours and would make a great place for them to live."

"This is all starting to make sense now," I replied.

Alex stated, "I must go now. I hope this has been a good day for you all. Keep up the excellent work and I'll see you all soon." He turned, took a few steps, and disappeared into a portal that we had no clue was there.

We all stood for a minute in silence, taking in everything that had just happened. We walked back to the truck and headed home without saying one word to one another. We were all overwhelmed.

31

SUMMERS END

The next morning, we woke to my mother having to shake us awake and saying, "Hey kids! Time for breakfast." We were so mentally exhausted from everything that Alex had shared with us. The world we live in is nothing that we thought it was at the start of summer. Everything that we thought was possible has now changed. We were no longer innocent kids that could just hang out and have an enjoyable time.

School is about to start, and we won't have time to adventure into the woods much. The daylight will also be getting shorter as well. It'll be dark when we get on our bus heading to school as well as getting dark by the time we get home, after school. There will be no way to get up the hill into the woods once the snow has started to pile up.

Tomorrow, Jimmy's and Lisa's families will be moving out and into their new homes. I'm happy for them and really do feel fortunate to have had so much time with both of them over the summer. I am struggling, knowing that tonight will be our last dinner together as a group. They are all family to me. I know they are just down the road and I'll see them at school but there was something special about waking up to so much excitement on a daily basis.

Jimmy's new house.

I'm sure it will take some time to adjust my life back to what it was at the beginning of summer when it was just my mother, father, and me.

I can say that I'm pretty sure that we had the most exciting summer by any kids anywhere in the world. For that I am very thankful. I made lifetime friends in Lisa, Jimmy and even Mr. Tucker. Not to mention Alex and his species. The four of us are looking forward to learning more about our worlds.

I'm not sure what the future will bring all of us but I'm excited and can't wait to see what next summer will bring. For now, my life will go back to normal. Well, I guess as normal as it can be. I'm sure that Lisa, Jimmy, Mr. Tucker and I will continue to make natural products, when we have time, that will benefit both of our worlds. Maybe even the Lizard people's world. I am still trying to digest that bit of information. That leaves us with another question. Are there more worlds that we have yet to discover?

After learning so many amazing secrets over the summer and having so many more questions for Alex, I'm sure that this is not the end but rather...

THE BEGINNING!

ABOUT THE AUTHOR

Jay Vernon grew up on a rural farm in Central Wisconsin in the late '60s through the mid-'80s. From there, he'd experience many strange and unusual things throughout those years, unforgettable sightings as a teenager in the deep woods where he spent so much of his time. He was always conscious and knew that there were dangerous animals in the woods of Adams County, but just not how much.

ALSO BY JAY VERNON

Adams County Bigfoot: Friend or Beast?

AFTERWORD

Go to hangar1publishing.com to learn more about the Authors and stay up to date with their newest releases.

www.ingramcontent.com/pod-product-compliance
Lightning Source LLC
Chambersburg PA
CBHW060139150626
46550CB00015B/2090